From Fear
to
Faith

〜 Matthew Allen

Published by
Spiritbuilding Publishing
15591 N. State Rd. 9
Summitville, IN 46070

Printed in the United States of America
FROM FEAR TO FAITH
by Matthew Allen

ISBN: 978-0-9829811-7-7

Cover:Emilea Allen, ©2014 Leslie Savage Photography

Spiritual "equipment" for the contest of life.

Spiritbuilding
Publishing

Acknowledgements

There are a number of Christians who have been instrumental in helping me come to a better understanding of the assurance and hope we have in Jesus. Over the last few years, men like **Daniel DeGarmo, Dave Roberts, Jim Grushon Jr., Jim Canada, Edwin Crozier,** and **Max Ray** have played a big role in shaping my understanding on this important subject. I will be forever thankful for the time and assistance these men have offered. And most of all, I am thankful for the eldership at Kettering Church of Christ in Kettering, Ohio, who has continually stood behind me in this project. The support and constant feedback of **Rich Walker, Russ Robins**, and **George Wacks** has been invaluable. I am honored that all three men have used this material in the teaching curriculum for our local church family. What you hold in your hands today would not have been possible without their encouragement.

I am also thankful for my wife **Becky Allen** who has done much of the grammatical editing of this work. Her patience and words of advice have been extremely helpful! God has blessed me with a wonderful spiritual companion.

I also appreciate **Carl McMurray** of SPIRITBUILDING PUBLISHING who ten years ago encouraged me to begin writing for him. As one of his former interns, I will forever be indebted to him for his instruction, advice, and godly example.

Table of Contents ⌒

Prologue

In 2006, **Dave Roberts,** who would later become one of the shepherds in the church at Brownsburg, Indiana, inspired me to delve into a subject that has changed my life forever. That is, the need for assurance in our salvation. Too many Christians approach their spiritual life with doubt and uncertainty. They do not know for sure they are saved. They feel they will never add up or be good enough for God. They wonder if they would **really** be saved if they were to die suddenly, or if the Lord were to return. While they responded in primary obedience to the gospel years before, they now find themselves given over to doubt as to whether they remain in a saved condition.

Have I done enough?

Have I kept all of the commands?

What if I have missed something in regards to my spiritual life?

Some feel that at one moment they are in salvation, and the next moment, out of salvation. Silently, they wonder whether God can forgive them for what has gone on in their life since their salvation.

Will God be patient with me as I deal with my shortcomings, repetitive sin, and even outright failures?

I know how that feels, because it is the way I used to live. I am so thankful for my good brother and spiritual mentor who first challenged me to rethink the paradigm I had been operating from. In the fall of 2006, I preached a series of lessons on this subject, which became the basis for a Bible class and this book. The first edition of *From Fear to Faith* has been bought by believers around the world. Since 2007, I have preached the message of the hope and assurance of our salvation around the United States and beyond. The reaction has been the same wherever I go. I usually hear something like:

We need more sermons like that…

I needed to hear that, because I just worry that I'm not good enough to be saved.

This inspires me to keep on keeping on. Having moved to Ohio in 2010, once again I've been blessed to work under a group of shepherds who have encouraged me to continue this pursuit.

As you will see, I approach this subject with passion. The message of the New Testament is one of hope and grace. In his prayer for the Romans Paul said, *May the God of hope fill you with all joy and peace in believing, so that by the power of the Holy Spirit you may abound in hope*, Romans 15.13. The apostles labored to explain our adoption as sons and daughters of God. They spoke often about the riches of our spiritual inheritance in the next life. For example:

- *For in Christ Jesus you are all sons of God, through faith*, Galatians 3.26.

- God wants to *show (us) the immeasurable riches of his grace in kindness toward us in Christ Jesus,* Ephesians 2.7.

- Peter wrote of an *imperishable, undefiled, and unfading* inheritance, *kept in heaven for you,* 1 Peter 1.3-4.

- John testified that when we sin we have an *Advocate* who pleads on our behalf, 1 John 1.7-2.3.

The Scriptures resoundingly affirm that **every** Christian can live with full assurance and trust God for their salvation. We need a healthy dose of faith in these Scriptures! God's word is true! We can trust our very soul on it. We are those who are *in hope of eternal life, which God, who never lies, promised before the ages began,* Titus 1.2.

Each Christian must learn to trust, not in his or her own perfection or works to merit salvation, but in the work of God. When we sin, God stands ready to forgive. We need to learn to forgive ourselves and understand that Christianity is a process. We stand, not in our strength, but in the strength of God, Ephesians 6.10-13. Faith is a journey, not a destination. Christians must never live as if they have "arrived." No person has ever lived the Christian life perfectly and no one has things all figured out. We are to be progressing and participating in the transformation process for the rest of our life. We must move with a spirit of humility and compassion for others, recognizing just how much God has forgiven us.

Why Is This a Problem in Today's Church?

Throughout the twentieth century, God's people rightfully defended God's truth against the false doctrine of *impossibility of apostasy.* Debate notes and long discourses about those whom we disagreed with filled our pulpits. However, there seems to have been little emphasis on God's assurance of our salvation. Please do not misunderstand. In our pulpits, there is a need for teaching that exposes false doctrine for what it is. *Calvinism* is not a biblical doctrine, primarily because it denies the freewill of mankind. We are freewill beings and have the ability to choose whom we will serve, before and after becoming a Christian. The Calvinistic doctrine of *impossibility of apostasy* denies this fact. Jesus' teaching in the parable of the Sower (Matthew 13, Mark 4), Simon the Sorcerer (Acts 8), teaching in Hebrews (Hebrews 2.1-3; 10.22-39), and Peter's writing (2 Peter 2.20-22), destroys the concept of *impossibility of apostasy.* We can willfully turn our back on God, walk away, and be lost.

But, this is the **last** thing many Christians intend to do. The vast majority never set out to reject God. But, temptation will come during moments of weakness, and sometimes we sin. To this, no Christian is immune. After succumbing to sin, some may wonder:

• *Has God really forgiven me ... even if I knew better when I engaged in sin?*

• *Did God really mean it when He promised to forgive me when I repent and confess my sin?*

• *I have struggled with repetitive sin. Have I run out of chances with God?*

How Do We Address the Problem?

We must equip Christians for the transformation process. Living as the new person God created is not without its battles with the flesh. See Romans 7. When we come to God for salvation, we must allow Him to go to work in our life. This involves full surrender, Galatians 2.20. Our power for survival and success lie in Him and the strength of His word, Romans 8.13; Ephesians 6.10, 13. We must resist the idea that we must be perfect in order to get to heaven. Any expectation of a Christian coming out of the baptistry water and never falling to temptation again should be steadfastly rejected.

We need to cultivate an atmosphere of encouragement. Local churches must focus on the importance of building strong relationships within their congregation. *Let us hold fast the confession of our hope without wavering, for He who promised is faithful. And let us consider how to stir up one another to love and good works, not neglecting to meet together, as is the habit of some, but encouraging one another, and all the more as you see the Day drawing near,* Hebrews 10.23-25. The focus must be on helping others along our journey toward heaven. *Love one another with brotherly affection. Outdo one another in showing honor. Do not be slothful in zeal, be fervent in spirit, serve the Lord. Rejoice in hope, be patient in tribulation, be constant in prayer. Contribute to the needs of the saints and seek to show hospitality. Bless those who persecute you; bless and do not curse them. Rejoice with those who rejoice, weep with those who weep. Live in harmony with one another,* Romans 12.10-16.

We need to cultivate an atmosphere of transparency. Do the members of your spiritual family feel comfortable communicating their personal struggles and setbacks? *Therefore, confess your sins to one another and pray for one another, that you may be healed. The prayer of a righteous person has great power as it is working,* James 5.16. How comfortable does the average Christian feel in sharing their burdens, mistakes, and temptations with others? Spiritual families are not a social club for those who have it all together and all figured out, because no one does. The church is a rescue station for sinners. God designed it to be a place of healing and safety. In some places, the weakest and most vulnerable Christians turn away too soon. This may be due to the creation of a sterile environment which leads to the impression that a person must be perfect, always able to say "no" to sin. Such places are discouraging. They make a person feel uncomfortable and intimidated.

How can I ever be good enough?

I'll never be perfect, so why try?

Congregations need to be mindful of the need for a helpful environment that recognizes the reality of fleshly weakness. We must commit to the work of helping people move away from their sin. This approach is positive and encouraging. The other is rooted in fear. A helpful environment builds up. The other tears down.

Imagine your congregation for a moment. Visualize some of the families who are present. Today, there is a good probability that there is:

- A husband who is fighting an internet pornography addiction and even though he tries with all his might, just cannot seem to kick the habit.

- A teenager who came to church today struggling with a decision on what to do about an out of wedlock pregnancy.

- A wife who is dealing with disenchantment in her marriage and herself. She is tempted to look to another man who shows interest in her and makes her happy about herself.

- A young man who is on the edge and feeling pressure to participate in the homosexual lifestyle.

- A couple who is tempted to cheat on their taxes.

- A middle aged person who feels they have made so many mistakes in life that they cannot possibly recover and be where they think they ought to be.

These are real problems being faced by real Christians everywhere. For those who struggle, an encouraging atmosphere is more conducive to spiritual growth and transformation. There is a huge difference between a message of hope, deliverance, and reliance on God's solutions to their problem and being told week after week they are not doing enough to obey God. Instead of learning about tools to help them cope with real life situations and problems, they feel surrounded by "perfect" people who have forgotten what it feels like to be so "imperfect."

Some Christians do not need to be reminded they fall short. They are very aware of their struggles. Will they receive the encouragement to wholeheartedly pursue Jesus despite their imperfections, Philippians 3.7-11? Is there an equipping for **real life** problems? Through the years, one of the saddest things I've witnessed is knowing of struggling Christians who sink further into the murky depths of despair, as others in the spiritual family turn on them, judging them for their shortcomings. There is no offer to help—it's just criticism. After so long, the weak one simply turns away. Spiritually, this is the act of "shooting our own." It is little wonder why some new converts are lost to the world.

Move with understanding that teaching on grace, forgiveness, and mercy is not advocating a soft gospel or "cheap grace." Critics often charge, *grace equals leniency.* Does it? Not at all. Grace is not a license to sin! It is our motivation **not to sin!** *For the grace of God has appeared, bringing salvation for all people, training us to renounce ungodliness and worldly passions, and to live self-controlled, upright, and godly lives in the present age, waiting for our blessed hope, the appearing of the glory of our great God and Savior Jesus Christ, who gave himself for us to redeem us from all lawlessness and to purify for himself a people for his own possession who are zealous for good works,* Titus 2.11-14.

Grace, forgiveness, mercy, and hope are biblical topics. Just because others in the religious world tie religious error to these theological concepts, does not mean we should ignore them. I find it tragic to have found so many

Christians who know little about God's grace and live with little assurance of salvation. Many possess a flawed viewpoint of God and do not know how to relate to Him other than through the perspective of law.

In *From Fear to Faith,* it is my desire to conduct an in-depth study on the assurance of our salvation. I want to help Christians find more hope, confidence, and trust in God. We must rest not in ourselves, but in the grace of God.

The Scriptures teach that Christians **were** saved, Romans 8.24; **are being** saved, 1 Corinthians 15.2; and **shall be** saved, Romans 5.9-10. Those who live in faith will be saved, wholly, completely, and forevermore! Challenge yourself each day to take God at His word and be thankful for His adopting you as His son or daughter. *Do not be afraid, little flock, for your Father has chosen gladly to give you the kingdom,* Luke 12.32.

How Could God Love Someone Like Me?

Introduction:

You know the feeling. It starts deep down inside. As it grows the gnawing in your stomach begins and anxiety builds. What feeling? It's the realization that you've messed up ... **again**. Satan sought out your weaknesses and effectively exploited them to the fullest. And now, the guilt. The constant questioning:

If only I had ...

Then there is the dread of coming to worship services and thinking:

If these people knew half the things I struggle with, they'd toss me out of here.

Many Christians begin their new life with zealousness and an intense desire to live right. But after so long, Satan comes calling and leads them back toward the same habits they had before their relationship with Christ. Out of weakness, they succumb to temptation. Sometimes the guilt is overpowering. Satan continually works, pressing hard to convince us that it is time to throw in the towel and give up.

There's no use. I'm just not cut out for this Christianity thing ...

For countless numbers of Christians, this scenario happens all the time.

The Danger of Perfectionism and Self-Comparison

The Hebrew writer likened sin to a great weight that ties us down, Hebrews 12.1. Sin paralyzes spiritual progress and shackles us with remorse. Then, as Jesus' perfect example of holiness comes into view, things can feel even worse. When Peter finally realized the true identity of Jesus, he responded, *Go away from me Lord, for I am a sinful man, O Lord,* Luke 5.8. There is a constant realization that **God** is holy and **we** are not.

Sometimes this burden feels overwhelming. This huge sense of despair and uncertainty must have been part of the thought process of those gathered together on the day of Pentecost. What a powerful, passionate sermon Peter gave! With no apologies, Peter delivered the painful reality to his audience. The Jews had crucified the Son of God, Acts 2.36. His listeners urgently asked, *Brethren, what shall we do?* They understood their guilt. They were lost and needed a means to be forgiven. Acts 2.38-42 records Peter's answer. About 3000 souls were added to the church that day.

The way out of sin is through Jesus. God's great desire is to pardon the sin of all people, Acts 17.30-31. To those who have never obeyed, like those in our example in Acts 2, they must submit to the terms of God's grace. Faith is generated by hearing the gospel, Romans 10.17. Faith is simply the action of a convicted heart which responds by reaching out to God. We reach out to Him in repentance. We surrender by removing ourselves off the throne of our heart, confessing Jesus as Lord (Romans 10.9-10) and dying with Christ in the waters of baptism, Romans 6.3-6. When we sin after our baptism, we are instructed to confess our sins and seek God's forgiveness, 1 John 1.8-10. **There can be no assurance of salvation while walking in darkness**. *Why do you call me Lord, Lord, and do not the things that I say?* Luke 6.46.

Human perfection in regard to any law (Old or New) is unattainable, Romans 3.9-10; Galatians 3.21. Satan works through the weakness of the flesh to subject us to temptation. We are not always at our strongest and will give in to sin. It is a constant struggle for every Christian. Paul wrestled with his flesh, Romans 7.14-25. Satan wants our soul back. After sinning, he tells us we are no longer worthy to be a Christian and there is no use in trying anymore. It is at this point that some choose to move deeper into darkness and embrace a lifestyle of sin. **Those who believe Satan and choose to willfully engage in sin through walking in darkness will not be saved**, Galatians 6.7-8.

We can add to our problems by comparing ourselves to others. It is very easy to observe other Christians and form an inaccurate image. We perceive they are so strong that when temptation comes it is summarily dismissed. We see fellow Christians who always have a smile on their face, are upbeat, happily married, busy in the work of the church, and know most of the answers in Bible class.

What are they doing that I'm not? Will I ever add up?

This mindset is deadly. Paul wrote, *Not that we dare to classify or compare ourselves with some of those who are commending themselves. But when they measure themselves by one another and compare themselves with one another, they are without understanding,* 2 Corinthians 10.12.

Self-comparison leads us down a road which leads to disappointment and ruin. **Everyone** struggles with sin. *All have sinned and fall short of the glory of God,* Romans 3.23. The cold, hard reality of this life is that God's sons and daughters will fall prey to sin and when we do, Jesus stands in our place, and makes propitiation for us. *If we say we have no sin, we deceive ourselves, and the truth is not in us. If we say we have not sinned, we make him a liar, and his word is not in us. My little children, I am writing these things to you so that you may not sin.* **But if anyone does sin, we have an advocate with the Father, Jesus Christ the righteous. He is the propitiation for our sins,** *and not for ours only but also for the sins of the whole world.* **And by this we know that we have come to know him, if we keep his commandments,** [emphasis mine] 1 John 1.8, 10; 2.1-3. Those who think they have it all together are still subject to weakness and sin.

Three Things We Can Do with Sin

I once read that there are three things we can do with sin.

- **We can resolve to never sin again**. This mentality is a setup for failure. Even though we must try, avoiding sin completely is impossible. See 1 John 1.8.

- **We can let sin make us a coward**. Think of Judas. When he realized the terrible consequences of his scheme, he went out and hanged himself, Matthew 27.3-5. He could have faced his sin through confessing it to God. God would have forgiven him. Instead, Judas listened to the lie of darkness and now has all eternity to deal with the regret of his sin. Sin turned Judas into a coward. Don't let sin make you a coward.

- **We must learn from our sin**; since resolving to never sin again and not facing our sin are ways leading to defeat. This is the third and most profitable option. It is what Peter did. After suffering a crushing spiritual defeat by denying Jesus three times (Matthew 26.69-75) the apostle sought God's forgiveness and picked himself up, John 21.15-19. A mere fifty days after the resurrection, Peter preached the greatest sermon of his life. Over 3000 repented and were baptized. It was a stunning turnaround for a person who walked through the deepest spiritual valley only two months before.

Toward the end of his life, Peter praised God.

> *Blessed be the God and Father of our Lord Jesus Christ, who according to His great mercy has caused us to be born again to a living hope through the resurrection of Jesus Christ from the dead, to obtain an inheritance which is imperishable and undefiled and will not fade away, reserved in heaven for you.*
>
> — 1 Peter 1.3-4

Peter knew all about mercy and forgiveness. He personally experienced it, John 21.15-17. What was true for Peter remains true for us. Our repentance brings mercy and forgiveness from God. When God says something, He means it. We must move in faith and learn to trust Him more. When God says it's over, it's over. *Repent therefore, and turn again, that your sins may be blotted out*, Acts 3.19. When God forgives, it is as if the sin never happened. It's been obliterated, destroyed, wiped out, never to be brought up again.

With God, It's Personal

God sent His Son to the cross to be the perfect sacrifice for sin. Jesus is our propitiation for sin, 1 John 2.2. Jesus died for everyone, Romans 15.17-19. It makes no difference how many sins have to be forgiven. No one is beyond

God's power to save. *He is able to save to the uttermost those who draw near to God through him, since he always lives to make intercession for them,* Hebrews 7.25. This passage makes it clear that **forgiveness is not a one-time event**. Jesus *always lives to make intercession for us.* He continues to be the offering that turns away God's wrath. We can always approach the Father, confess our sin, and be assured that He will **always** welcome us back into His grace, 1 John 1.7-9.

While we will cover this more in depth later in this book, some may wonder about sins and shortcomings they can't presently see or recognize. Every Christian is in a growing process, 2 Peter 1.5-11. Looking back at your life you may see shortcomings and sins that you committed previously that you only now have come to recognize with growth and maturity in Christ. Does this mean you were not saved then? While we must never be content with our weaknesses, we must also leave room for God's patience, grace, and mercy. Our Father understands our situation perfectly. He knows every circumstance. He knows our heart. He knows we are in the midst of a process of growth and maturation. There is no one who God wishes to be lost, 2 Peter 3.9. See what the Holy Spirit says a little later in the chapter: *Therefore, beloved, since you are waiting for these, be diligent to be found by him without spot or blemish, and at peace.* **And count the patience of our Lord as salvation,** *just as our beloved brother Paul also wrote to you according to the wisdom given him. But grow in the grace and knowledge of our Lord and Savior Jesus Christ. To Him be the glory both now and to the day of eternity. Amen,* [emphasis mine] 2 Peter 3.14-15, 18.

God sees the big picture. He is our Heavenly Father and thrives on giving us time to grow and become stronger. While we must never take His patience for granted, knowledge of this fact should bring us great comfort. Consider how Jesus handled the constant setbacks of the apostles. They struggled in understanding the concept and scope of the kingdom—even up to the night before Jesus' death. Jesus' impending death and the spiritual nature of His kingdom were a constant theme in Jesus' ministry. Yet, they just could not fully grasp God's entire plan. Not once do we see Jesus casting them off and giving up on them. He constantly gave them new chances to learn and apply the knowledge. **God will not give up on us**! Through the Spirit, He constantly offers His help as we navigate through life – and learn more about Him. He is patient and He wants us to achieve the highest possible good.

This may be a different picture of the Father than we are used to. Far too many Christians have an inaccurate viewpoint of God. Often, Jesus is viewed as the One who is loving, compassionate, and ready to dispense grace. The Father is viewed as judgmental, vengeful, and one ready to dispense punishment at a moment's notice. Some feel they may never be able to win with their Heavenly Father. Yet, it is Jesus, who told Philip, *Whoever has seen me has seen the Father*, John 14.9b. Just as Jesus is, so is the Father. They share the same desire. God is on our side and wants our salvation. It is His good pleasure to do so. It was the Father who *raised up a horn of salvation for us in the house of his servant David … that we, being delivered from the hand of our enemies, might serve him without fear, in holiness and righteousness before him all our days*, Luke 1.69, 74-75.

The *horn of salvation* in Luke 1.69 is Jesus, our Savior. Note that it was the Father's desire to rescue (deliver) us from sin so that we can serve Him **without fear**, 1.74. It is simply impressive to see the message of assurance and hope woven throughout the Bible. In both well-known and obscure passages the message is the same: God's love, care, and concern for us is immeasurable! **The Father longs for our salvation!**

Conclusion:

Heaven is not an unattainable goal. It is not the destination of so called "super-Christians." It is the destination of those who have been forgiven and stand by the grace of God. Because of the abundant mercy of God, we have a *living hope* of salvation given to us through the resurrection of Jesus from the dead. What a wonderful source of motivation for us as we go through life! God will go to whatever depth and any length to save us.

Regular meditation on these facts will radically change your life. The reality is: **God does love someone like you!**

For Thought and Reflection:

1. To what did the Hebrew writer liken sin? What are its effects?

2. What is Satan's role in tempting Christians to sin?

3. How do passages such as Romans 3.23 and 1 John 1.8-10; 2.1-3 help you as you struggle with spiritual shortcomings or setbacks?

4. What are three things we can do with sin?

5. How did Peter deal with crushing spiritual defeat? How can this be a source of inspiration to you?

6. In Hebrews 7.15, what message is communicated to us?

7. What can we learn about deity's patience in how Jesus dealt with the apostles?

8. Have you ever possessed a negative view of God the Father? If so, how did you change your perspective?

9. How can knowledge of the Father's great love for you revolutionize your spiritual life?

10. What are three points you can write down to help you live with increased assurance in your spiritual life?

God's Amazing Forgiveness

Introduction:

We need regular reminders on God's forgiveness. A better understanding of God's mindset toward His creation will go far in helping us develop a stronger assurance of salvation. When we learn the lengths God has gone to save us from sin, it will serve as a motivator in day-to-day service and bolster our thankfulness. Many non-Christians feel they are too far gone to be saved. They believe they are out of reach by the hand of God. Some New Testament Christians get down after battling repetitive sin and feel they may have slipped one too many times to be forgiven **again**.

Our Father is the God who forgives. He lives to pardon mankind from sin. *Let the wicked forsake his way, and the unrighteous man his thoughts; let him return to the LORD, that he may have compassion on him, and to our God, for he will abundantly pardon,* Isaiah 55.7. Micah said: *Who is a God like you, pardoning iniquity and passing over transgression for the remnant of his inheritance? He does not retain his anger forever, because he delights in steadfast love,* Micah 7.18. In the New Testament, we read that God is: *Not slow to fulfill His promise as some count slowness, but is patient toward you, not wishing that any should perish, but that all should reach repentance,* 2 Peter 3.9.

Why has the Lord delayed in sending Jesus for His return? Could it be that God is still holding out for humanity to repent and turn from sin? He desires a relationship with His creation. And while we do not know when He will return (Matthew 24.36) each day is an opportunity for us to teach others about God's forgiveness.

> *If a wicked person turns away from all his sins that he has committed and keeps all My statutes and does what is just and right, he shall surely live; he shall not die. None of the transgressions that he has committed shall be remembered against him; for the righteousness that he has done he shall live. Have I any pleasure in the death of the wicked, declares the Lord GOD, and not rather that he should turn from his way and live?*
> — Ezekiel 18.21-23

God does not desire the death of the wicked because He loves them. God is holding out for the lost to be saved.

It is OK to think of and be thankful for the love of God. In fact, we should think of it more often. How much time do we spend in praise? We should be enthusiastic in sharing the good news of God's love with everyone we meet. Our friends need to hear a message of hope and optimism. They need to know that God loves them enough to forgive them of whatever they have done. When we realize just how much we have been forgiven, it motivates us to serve God with optimism, thankfulness, and hope. And as this disposition fills our life, our sharing the powerful message of grace will happen with **everyone** we meet.

As you read through the following examples of God's amazing forgiveness, ask yourself if these individuals would have been enthusiastic about what God did for them. You will see that thankfulness and appreciation for God would have poured from of their lips.

Manasseh, King of Judah

Manasseh's reign of 55 years over Judah is the longest of any king in the northern or southern kingdom. Manasseh's father, Hezekiah, was a godly king who initiated reform throughout Judah. Manasseh would have been a firsthand witness to the power of God as He twice delivered Judah from the hand of the Assyrians. The most notable example is seen in Isaiah 37 where God smote 185,000 members of the Assyrian army. Manasseh would have grown up seeing His father's total reliance upon Yahweh and would have been schooled by the prophets Isaiah and Micah.

But yet, Manasseh not only served idols, he ran as far away as he could from God. 2 Kings 21 gives us a comprehensive summary of his sin. Manasseh:

- *Rebuilt the high places ... and erected altars for Baal and made an Asherah ...and worshiped all the host of heaven and served them* (21.3).

- *Built altars in the house of the Lord.* And, he *built altars for all the host of heaven in the two courts of the house of the Lord* (21.4-5).

- *Made his son pass through the fire, practiced witchcraft and used divination, and dealt with mediums and spiritists* (21.6). Manasseh had more than one son. 2 Chronicles 33.6 says that he made his *sons* pass through the fire.

- *Set the carved image of Asherah … in the house of the Lord* (21.7).

- *Shed very much innocent blood until he had filled Jerusalem from one end to another* (21.16).

All these things provoked God to anger. Even worse, Manasseh led and seduced the people to follow him into a level of sin worse than the Canaanites. It was the sins of Manasseh that caused God to make the decision to have Judah destroyed, 21.11-12.

Jewish tradition says that the prophet Isaiah died at the hands of Manasseh, who had him sawn in two.[1] Could Hebrews 11.37 refer to Isaiah in the year 680 BC? Shortly after Isaiah's death, Manasseh joined the Ethiopians in a rebellion against Assyria. Assyria shut down the rebellion and placed Manasseh and the Ethiopian king, Tirhaka, into custody. The Assyrians *captured Manasseh with hooks and bound him with chains of bronze and brought him to Babylon,* 2 Chronicles 33.11b. Here he remained for twelve years, until the end of the reign of Esarhaddon. Here he would have remained, but there is a specific reason as to why Manasseh was released.

> *When he was in distress, he entreated the favor of the LORD his God and humbled himself greatly before the God of his fathers. He prayed to him, and God was moved by his entreaty and heard his plea and brought him again to Jerusalem into his kingdom. Then Manasseh knew that the LORD was God.*
>
> — 2 Chronicles 33.12-13

God forgave Manasseh! It's just an incredible story! Manasseh was the man whose sin brought the downfall of a nation. But not only did God forgive him, He also restored him to his kingdom and gave him twenty more years to rule Judah. 2 Chronicles 33.14-16 notes all the reform Manasseh initiated. Manasseh's heart had changed and his desire to serve the Lord was the direct result of God's willingness to forgive. How enthusiastic and grateful to God would Manasseh have been during the last two decades of his life? When he looked at the scars from his imprisonment, he would have known the hooks had been removed only because of the power of a loving and compassionate God.

Saul of Tarsus

Saul stands out as the great New Testament example of the lengths our God is willing to go to extend forgiveness. Before becoming a Christian, his life is well documented. In Philippians 3, Saul described himself as the Hebrew of Hebrews, rising to the top of the sect of the Pharisees. He had been trained in the best schools of learning and had garnered the respect of his peers. Saul was so zealous for Judaism that he became a leader in the arrests and persecution of the early Christians. In recounting his former life he said: *I not only locked up many of the saints in prison after receiving authority from the chief priests, but when they were put to death I cast my vote against them. And I punished them often in all the synagogues and tried to make them blaspheme, and in raging fury against them I persecuted them even to foreign cities,* Acts 26.10-11. There is little doubt that Saul played a major role in spearheading the great persecution that led to the scattering of the saints. He approved of the execution of Stephen, Acts 8.1. It was Saul who *ravaged the church, and entering house after house, he dragged off men and women and committed them to prison,* Acts 8.3.

Yet, Saul was forgiven! After receiving the gospel, Saul repented and was baptized, Acts 22.16. He willingly forsook religious traditions and practices that he knew were no longer pleasing to God. Now he lived by faith. *I have been crucified with Christ. It is no longer I who live, but Christ who lives in me. And the life I now live in the flesh I live by faith in the Son of God, who loved me and gave himself for me,* Galatians 2.20.

Now in his new life, Saul was commissioned by Jesus to become an apostle with the mission of preaching to the Gentiles, Galatians 1.16; Acts 9.15. Later, he was given the name Paul. Although the memory of his former life would continue to haunt him (1 Timothy 1.12-15) Paul trusted in the forgiveness and wonderful grace of God. Paul knew he had been forgiven and this knowledge propelled him to tremendous service for God. He was not hampered by fear or anxiety about salvation. He knew it was his, despite what he did before becoming a Christian. Paul rejoiced that *the grace of our Lord overflowed for me with the faith and love that are in Christ Jesus*, 1 Timothy 1.14.

The Prodigal Son

A powerful example in seeing God's willingness to forgive sons and daughters inside His family is found in Luke 15.11-32. The younger son requested his inheritance early. There could not have been a greater insult. He was rejecting his father completely. When he received it, he went far away and squandered his life. Things became so bad for him that he had no place to go and resorted to the lowest of jobs for a Jew—feeding swine. See his downward progression. He drifted from a comfortable home, surrounded by loved ones, to where he was completely alone, being forced to eat food fit only for farm animals. He could sink no further. **Finally**, he determined to come home.

Luke 15.20-24 is one of the most beautiful pictures of forgiveness in all of Scripture. Imagine the young man as he approaches his father's property. He is tired, unkempt, and dirty. His clothes are ragged and smell. Imagine his extreme embarrassment! He has resolved to go back to his father, acknowledge his sin, and seek to be as a hired servant. Instead of a harsh, judgmental response, the father runs to greet him, embraces him, and kisses him, 15.20. This is the way God reacts when His child returns. God leaps to His feet and runs to meet us! He is filled with joy when we renew our relationship with Him.

One of the things that makes the story in Luke 15 so powerful is that we have the picture of full restoration. The prodigal son insulted his father. He brought dishonor to the family. He wasted his physical blessings. Yet, when the son returned with a repentant heart, the father killed the fattened calf and held a celebration. The son only requested to become as one of his father's servants, yet the father fully restored his rightful place in the family – right along with everyone else. Fellowship was restored as if it had never been lost.

May we realize that **we are the prodigal son!** If there have been such seasons of sin in our lives and we have come home with a spirit of humble repentance, God has fully restored us to our place in His family. Remembering where we've come from helps us remain humble and vigilant as others struggle with sins of the flesh. See Galatians 6.1-2.

God Will Forgive You of Your Sin

Come now, let us reason together, says the LORD: *though your sins are like scarlet, they shall be as white as snow; though they are red like crimson, they shall become like wool,* Isaiah 1.18. We are each extreme examples of God's forgiveness. Sin separates us from God (Romans 3.23) and brings us spiritual death, Romans 6.23. Because of this, God sent His son to die for us. When we respond to God's terms of grace, we are added to the family of God. Even if we drift from God after coming into His family, we can be forgiven and fully restored.

Conclusion:

When God forgives us, we must forgive ourselves. There is no profit to beating up oneself. Our debt has been cancelled. We must not continue to live in fear. What God promises to do, He will do, Romans 8.14-16. Move forward in humble faith, placing all of your trust in God. Learn to depend on God. Approach your spiritual life with passionate enthusiasm and joy.

Our worldly friends need to see the power of a changed life. When we live with assurance, our entire outlook on life and willingness to share the gospel with others radically changes for the better.

For Thought and Reflection:

1. Read Isaiah 55.7; Micah 7.18, and 2 Peter 3.9. List three principles we can take from these passages.

2. Do you feel many New Testament Christians are less than enthusiastic about their salvation? Why?

3. What is one reason God has yet to send His Son to return?

4. Name three of what you think were Manasseh's most egregious sins.

5. Ultimately, what did the sins of Manasseh lead to? (2 Kings 21.11)

6. During the last years of his life, how grateful and zealous for God would Manasseh have been?

7. In 1 Timothy 1, how did Paul describe his former life?

8. After his obedience to the gospel, would you say Paul lived by fear or faith? Why? Use Scriptures to prove your example.

9. How did the father greet the prodigal son? What message does this send to us?

The Abundant Mercy of God

Introduction:

> *For You, Lord, are good, and ready to forgive,*
> *and abundant in loving-kindness to all who call upon You.*
>
> — Psalm 86.5

The Psalms express our deepest needs to a God that is ever present and always ready to come to our aid. Passage after passage testifies that God is concerned about us individually. Through His great mercy, He is committed to helping us navigate through every day of life. Without mercy, we could never approach God, never seek His face, never depend on Him, and never call Him our Father.

Psalm 86 was written during a time of trouble for David. While we are not exactly sure as to what situation he faced, it appears that he found himself physically threatened, 86.14. Under the direst of circumstances, we see David calling on God's character, appealing to God's mercy and grace. Whatever was going on at this point, David needed God's mercy more than anything. *Be gracious to me, O Lord, for to you do I cry all the day*, Psalm 86.3. David expresses his confidence in God's steadfast love and faithfulness, 86.15. Here, bold requests are made of God. David asks for God to use His strength and power to give him an advantage over his enemies. *Give your strength to your servant, and save the son of your maidservant*, 86.16. What may be amazing to us is that David did not hesitate in making this appeal to God. He had every confidence that God would grant his request because he had seen God do this time and time before. *In the day of my trouble I call upon you, for you answer me*, Psalm 86.7.

After his sin with Bathsheba, David's life was full of turmoil. He was chased and threatened, and was no stranger to danger. At one point, his own son tried to kill him, 2 Samuel 15-16. This was a time in David's life where he had to endure the chastening of God. These difficult circumstances were the consequences of his own sin. But instead of giving up and remaining in the pit of doubt and discouragement, David continually reached out to

God. He knew that God would respond with the same tenderness that a parent shows his child when in distress. We too, should be confident to approach God boldly.

> *Since then we have a great high priest who has passed through the heavens, Jesus, the Son of God, let us hold fast our confession. For we do not have a high priest who is unable to sympathize with our weaknesses, but one who in every respect has been tempted as we are, yet without sin. Let us then with confidence draw near to the throne of grace, that we may receive mercy and find grace to help in time of need.*
>
> — Hebrews 4.14-16

God is always ready to dispense His mercy upon us when we approach Him with a humble and contrite heart. In fact, God delights in **liberally** dispensing His mercy. In both Testaments there is a language of abundance when referencing God's love, mercy, and compassion. *He does not deal with us according to our sins, nor repay us according to our iniquities. For as high as the heavens are above the earth, so great is his steadfast love toward those who fear him; as far as the east is from the west, so far does he remove our transgressions from us,* Psalm 103.10-12. *In him we have redemption through his blood, the forgiveness of our trespasses, according to the riches of his grace, which he lavished upon us, in all wisdom and insight … But God, being rich in mercy, because of the great love with which he loved us,* Ephesians 1.7-8; 2.4.

In Ephesians 3, Paul prayed that the Ephesians may be able to grasp the *breadth and length and height and depth and to know the love of Christ, which surpasses knowledge,* 3.18-19. As you meditate on these passages, please note that **God is not stingy in pouring out His blessings on His children**. God has never begrudged any gift to mankind. God's mercy is without limit. No one is beyond His saving power.

The Difference between Grace and Mercy

While grace and mercy are closely connected, they are not the same thing. In making His grace available to us, **God gives us what we do not**

deserve. Grace relates to guilt. Grace is seen when picturing the guilty sinner standing before God, the all-knowing and powerful Judge. It is a judicial concept that forgives a crime. Our actions do not merit salvation. Grace involves a free gift. In giving salvation, God gives it to us without any consideration of our character at the time. God sent Jesus to die on the cross *while we were enemies,* Romans 5.10. *In this is love, not that we have loved God, but that he loved us and sent his Son to be the propitiation for our sins,* 1 John 4.10. It is easy to see that God demonstrated His grace in the giving of His Son, and ultimately through our salvation from sin.

Mercy is God's favor that **holds back from us what we deserve**. Mercy relates to misery. It is a product of strong affection, compassion, and pity. When God dispenses mercy, we need to develop a consciousness that a more negative treatment should have been justly dealt out. Mercy relates **to the condition of the sinner** in his sin. Mercy is "kindness and goodwill toward the miserable and afflicted, joined with a desire to relieve them."[2] Here is a wonderful passage that is an expression of praise for God's mercy: *Bless the LORD, O my soul, and forget not all his benefits, who forgives all your iniquity, who heals all your diseases, who redeems your life from the pit, who crowns you with steadfast love and mercy,* Psalm 103.2-4.

It is we who were inside the pit. We put ourselves there through our own sin and transgression. There was no escape. We rightly deserved to remain in the pit, because the justice of God demands it. But yet, God is also motivated by love and compassion to act with mercy. *…At an acceptable time, O God, in the abundance of your steadfast love answer me in your saving faithfulness. Deliver me from sinking in the mire; let me be delivered from my enemies and from the deep waters. Let not the flood sweep over me, or the deep swallow me up, or the pit close its mouth over me,* Psalm 69.13-15. Because of **God's actions**, we have been raised from a dirty cesspool of sin to be cleansed. Praise be to God for His great mercy! We have been adopted as sons and daughters of God and clothed with righteousness, Galatians 3.26-27. Our salvation is *not by works done by us in righteousness,* Titus 3.5a.

A powerful example of mercy is seen in Isaiah 43.22-24. Note the passage. Israel had not honored God. In fact, they had *burdened (God) with their sins* and *wearied (God) with (their) iniquities.* The number of their sins was innumerable. Since the beginning of their existence, Israel had continually sinned against God. They deserved to be destroyed for their sin. Yet God said, *I, I am he who blots out your transgressions for my own sake, and I will not remember your sins,* Isaiah 43.25.

See also Psalm 130.1–7.

The Key to Receiving Mercy

For those who approach God with a contrite and humble heart, **mercy is guaranteed**. The person outside of Christ comes realizing salvation comes only through God and His working. This involves a surrendering to His word and work. When we do, God will *regenerate us* through a washing, Titus 3.5c. *Regeneration* means to be "born again," or "to receive new life." **Only God does this.** Jesus said, *"Truly, truly, I say to you, unless one is born of water and the Spirit, he cannot enter the kingdom of God,* John 3.5. When God's kindness, goodness, and mercy moves us to believe in His promise of deliverance and we follow His instructions on how to receive it, He *regenerates* us. This happens through the process of *washing,* Titus 3.5c. This term is used throughout the New Testament—referencing the wiping out of sin, sanctification, cleansing, and purity. Acts 22.16 ties in "washing" with baptism. This is the moment when God moves and saves us.

From this point forward we move inside the process of sanctification and transformation. This does not occur in the absence of human weakness and occasional sin. When we recognize we have missed the mark, and seek God's forgiveness, God will blot out the transgression. **We need to believe the Bible.** We must take it for face value and trust what it says. *Blessed are the poor in spirit, for theirs is the kingdom of heaven. Blessed are those who mourn, for they shall be comforted. Blessed are the meek, for they shall inherit the earth. Blessed are those who hunger and thirst for righteousness, for they* *shall be satisfied*, Matthew 5.3-6. Christians, who are poor in spirit, mourn over sin, and are meek and hungry for righteousness, will receive mercy.

Again, this is all contingent on bending our heart to God's way. We must move in His direction. We cannot have it both ways. Many want, and some demand, God's mercy, but do not want to do what God says. I am reminded of the Old Testament prophet, Balaam, who gained fame because of his incredible stubbornness. Not until a donkey spoke to him did he see the need to listen to God. He said, *Let me die the death of the upright, and let my end be like his*, Numbers 23.10b. "Balaam wanted to die like the righteous, but did not want to live like the righteous. God offers mercy, but mercy must be accepted on God's terms."[3]

Have you surrendered your heart?

Conclusion:

We have so much to be thankful for. Our sin has been enormous, but God's mercy is great. Our sin has driven a wedge between God and us, yet His mercy is always available. Those who come to Him are promised to become His sons and daughters. What a great God we have!

For Thought and Reflection:

1. To what did David appeal to during his time of distress?

2. Do we often approach God as boldly as David did? Why? Why not?

3. Besides the ones listed in the lesson, can you think of additional Scripture references that speak of the abundant mercy of God?

4. Define grace. What are two passages that help us more effectively understand grace?

5. Define mercy.

6. What prompts God to act in mercy?

7. What is key in receiving mercy?

8. What is promised to those who follow Jesus' instructions in Matthew 5:3-6?

9. What can we learn from Balaam's attitude?

A Deeper Appreciation for Grace

Introduction:

> *Grace is the soul of the gospel; without it the gospel is dead. Grace is the music of the gospel; without it the gospel is silent as to all comfort.*[4]

Throughout Scripture the repeated message we so often see is that our **God is a saving God**. Our God yearns for closeness with His creation. He wishes to redeem us from sin and bring us into a relationship with Him. His power to save is seen over and over again. These passages are just a few examples:

- **Titus 1.3** — *God our Savior.*

- **Titus 1.4** — *God the Father and Christ Jesus our Savior.*

- **Titus 2.10** — *God our Savior.*

- **Titus 3.4** — *God our Savior.*

- **Titus 3.6** — *Jesus Christ our Savior.*

- See also Matthew 20.28; Luke 19.10; 1 Timothy 2.5-6.

God's desire to save is purely an act of grace. He willingly gave the closest and dearest part of Him to make a relationship with Him possible. *For God so loved the world, that He gave His only Son, that whoever believes in Him should not perish but have eternal life,* John 3.16. Had God not acted through sending Jesus to be our propitiation, we would be hopelessly lost and destined for eternal condemnation. *For by grace you have been saved through faith. And this is not your own doing; it is the gift of God, not a result of works, so that no one may boast,* Ephesians 2.8-9.

As we seek to define grace, we could easily sum it up in one word: **Jesus**. Paul wrote, *for the grace of God has appeared, bringing salvation for all people,* Titus 2.11. The first part of this verse mentions an appearing. What appeared? Grace. How and when did it appear? We get the answer to our question by looking at Luke 1.79 where Jesus is described as light breaking out in the darkness *to guide our feet into the way of peace.* "Grace" is personified as Jesus. God *saved us and called us to a holy calling, not because of our works but because of His own purpose and grace, which He gave us in Christ Jesus before the ages began, and which now has been manifested through the **appearing** of our Savior Christ Jesus, who abolished death and brought life and immortality to light through the gospel,* 2 Timothy 1.9-10 [emphasis mine]. The coming of grace is also described as God's *goodness* and *loving kindness*, Titus 3.4. And finally, we look to John's gospel where he testified to seeing Jesus' glory, ... *glory as of the only Son from the Father, **full of grace and truth** ... for from his fullness we have all received, grace upon grace,* John 1.14, 16 [emphasis mine].

When it comes to our redemption, we owe everything to Jesus. Titus 2.11 says Jesus brought salvation. Through Him comes redemption and deliverance from Satan's bondage. Jesus was "literally laden with salvation. He didn't come sparingly, He was loaded with it."[5] Paul wrote that God *desires **all people** to be saved,* so He sent Jesus *who gave Himself as a ransom for all,* 1 Timothy 2.4, 6 [emphasis mine]. Ephesians 1.7 and 2.4-7 are filled with the language of abundance. God desires to save the worst of sinners!

So what will we do with grace? What will we do about Jesus? The answer to this question comes down to faith. Will we believe in His power to save? Will we respond in faith to His terms of receiving grace? If we wish to escape hell and live in heaven, there is no other choice. The answer is not found in ourselves. The answer is found in God. Not only does God want us to reach out to Him, He pleads with us to lean on Him in total dependence. When Jesus was asked about the greatest commandment in the Law, He said, *You shall love the Lord your God with all your heart and with all your soul and with all your mind. This is the great and first commandment,* Matthew 22.36-38.

The Essentialness of Grace

When we speak of grace, we refer to the work of God through Jesus to bring us salvation. Our salvation is only possible because of the grace of God. I like Jay Lockhart's excellent summary of grace and share it with you here:

- The **gospel** is *the gospel of the grace of God,* Acts 20.24.

- We **stand** in grace, Romans 5.1-2.

- We are **sustained** by grace, 2 Corinthians 12.9.

- We **serve** God by grace, Hebrews 12.28.

- We have **assurance** because of grace, 2 Thessalonians 2.16-17.

- We are **enabled** by grace, Acts 4.33.

- Jesus is God's **gift** of grace to us, Hebrews 2.9; 2 Corinthians 9.15.

- We have **become what we are in Christ** by grace, 1 Corinthians 15.10.[6]

When asked to define grace, most would quickly say that it is God's "unmerited favor." By expressing His grace, God gives us what we do not deserve: forgiveness of sin, a relationship with Him, and ultimately, an eternal home with Him in heaven. The New Testament writers labored to explain to us God's desire for our salvation.

- *But we see him who for a little while was made lower than the angels, namely Jesus, crowned with glory and honor because of the suffering of death, so that by the grace of God he might taste death for everyone,* Hebrews 2.9. God allowed Jesus to taste death for everyone so that we might live eternally.

- God was *rich in mercy, because of the great love with which he loved us, even when we were dead in our trespasses, made us alive together with Christ—by grace you have been saved,* Ephesians 2.4-5.

Those who choose to accept God's grace deserve death, but are given glory and honor. We were dead in our trespasses, but have been made alive with Christ, Colossians 2.13. These gifts have been given to us by the free will of God. God was not coerced, manipulated, or pressured into grace. It is an expression of who He is. It is a result of His unlimited love.

In this the love of God was made manifest among us, that God sent his only
Son into the world, so that we might live through him. In this is love, not that
we have loved God but that he loved us and sent his Son to be the propitiation
for our sins. Beloved, if God so loved us, we also ought to love one another. No
one has ever seen God; if we love one another, God abides in us and his love
is perfected in us. By this we know that we abide in him and he in us, because
he has given us of his Spirit. And we have seen and testify that the Father has
sent his Son to be the Savior of the world. Whoever confesses that Jesus is the
Son of God, God abides in him, and he in God. So we have come to know and
to believe the love that God has for us. God is love, and whoever abides in love
abides in God, and God abides in him. By this is love perfected with us, so
that we may have confidence for the day of judgment, because as he is so also
are we in this world. There is no fear in love, but perfect love casts out fear. For
fear has to do with punishment, and whoever fears has not been perfected in
love.

—1 John 4.9–18

Hebrews 2.9 and Romans 5.6–10 testify that Jesus died as our substitute.
He suffered the penalty that was really ours—**death**. The following
principle expressed by a fellow gospel preacher has helped me greatly in
developing my understanding of grace.

> When we forgive someone, we have to take the punishment. When
> someone does you wrong, if you take the idea that you must be paid for
> whatever is lost before the record is settled, this is not forgiveness. True
> forgiveness is when one is willing to 'bear the cost' and say, 'I'll just take
> the hurt on me.' 'You have hurt me, but I will take it; I forgive you.' "Sin is
> against God, but God takes the beating in that He sent Jesus to die to pay
> the price for OUR sin.[7]

God has most certainly given us what we do not deserve. It is because of the
blood of Christ we stand! *God counts righteousness apart from works: 'Blessed*
are those whose lawless deeds are forgiven, and whose sins are covered; blessed is
the man against whom the Lord will not count his sin,' Romans 4.6–8.

What Grace Is Not

While we stand in Christ through grace, it is essential that we understand what is not involved in God's grace. **Grace is not a license to sin.** *What shall we say then? Are we to continue in sin that grace may abound? By no means! How can we who died to sin still live in it?* Romans 6.1–2. Grace is not something to be taken for granted, and we must not use it as a crutch in justifying weakness. While God is patient with us as we work through our weaknesses and struggles, He simply will not allow us to slack off on needed areas of improvement. God calls for diligence in putting on the new character, 2 Peter 1.5–11; 3.14.

Grace is not based on human performance. God's divine favor has been granted despite the fact our condition was reprehensible before He saved us. There are no human works of merit capable of making us right before God. We simply cannot work ourselves to heaven. Period. **This is true** *before* **salvation and** *after* **salvation**. Every human being is always in need of God's grace. *For all have sinned and fall short of the glory of God,* Romans 3.23. *God shows his love for us in that while we were still sinners, Christ died for us. Since, therefore, we have now been justified by his blood, much more shall we be saved by him from the wrath of God. For if while we were enemies we were reconciled to God by the death of his Son, much more, now that we are reconciled, shall we be saved by his life,* Romans 5.8–10.

Grace is not cheap. In Bonhoefer's book, *The Cost of Discipleship,* we find a good definition of "cheap" grace:

> (This is) the justification of sin without the justification of the sinner. Grace alone does everything, they say, and so everything can remain as it was before. ... Cheap grace is the preaching of forgiveness without requiring repentance, baptism without church discipline, communion without confession, absolution without personal confession. Cheap grace is grace without discipleship, grace without the cross, grace without Jesus Christ, living and incarnate.[8]

Salvation is not acquired passively. Some expect little or nothing out of those who come to Jesus.

> "In much of Evangelicalism, the flippant sort of 'once saved, always saved' mentality, which denies that true grace will always prove itself in faith and works, is closely related to an 'easy-believism' mindset, which suggests that intellectual belief alone, which does not go on to pursue a life of true holiness, is the kind of faith that saves."[9]

We must not confuse "cheap" with "free." God's gift of grace was offered for free—Jesus paid the price. *You were ransomed from the futile ways inherited from your forefathers, not with perishable things such as silver or gold, but with the precious blood of Christ, like that of a lamb without blemish or spot,* 1 Peter 1.18-19. Since such a great price was paid on our behalf, let us wholeheartedly embrace God's grace and what it requires. "What cost God so much cannot be cheap for us."[10]

How Do You Relate to the Father?

Grace will be anything but cheap when we relate to the Father in the way He desires. In Luke 15, Jesus tells a series of parables to counter the accusations of the Pharisees who objected to His eating with tax collectors and sinners. When Jesus healed people with grave diseases, it was like a shepherd going out to find lost sheep, 15.3-7. When Jesus treated tax collectors as fellow human beings, it was like a woman seeking a lost coin, 15.8-10. When Jesus ate with sinners, it was like the Father heartily receiving the repentant prodigal son who wasted his inheritance with loose living, 15.11-32.

The last part of the parable of the prodigal son, 15.24-32, is designed to address all who tend to look on "sinners" with suspicion and contempt. The older son stood on the porch, outside the door where a celebration was being held in honor of his brother who had returned home with a repentant heart. The father killed the fattened calf, dressed his son in fine robes, and invited the entire family to come rejoice together. The older son was bitter, jealous, and filled with resentment. … *Look, these many years I have **served** you, and I never disobeyed your **command**, yet you never gave me a young goat, that I might celebrate with my friends. But when this son of yours came, who has devoured your property with prostitutes, you killed the fattened calf for him,* Luke 15:29-30 [emphasis mine].

You may be wondering why I chose to bold "served" and "command." I believe they are indicative of the attitude the older son possessed. In his perspective, he viewed himself as a *servant*. His father was his *master*. To him his father was more of an **issuer of commands** instead of a **loving father**. Now, make a personal application. How do you see your heavenly Father? He is so much more than a commander. He is your Father. He loves and cares for you and desires for you to relate to Him in that way.

God should never be viewed from a master/slave/works mindset. The Pharisees lived by this twisted perspective and it alienated them from everyone. They boasted in their works. *I fast twice a week, I pay tithes of all I get,* Luke 18.12. When we relate to God as slave to master, on the basis of hard work or obedience to a checklist of requirements, we will constantly live in fear and never grasp the dynamics of grace.

There must always be a provision made for God's grace.

Conclusion:

The Lord, the Lord God, is compassionate and gracious, slow to anger, and abounding in lovingkindness and truth, Exodus 34.6. *For of His fullness we have all received grace upon grace,* John 1.16. How do you view God? Too many have the mental image of God being the righteous judge, sitting high above, always angry with us when we fail to match up to His expectations. When we do not measure up, we crumble under the pressure because we feel we may have blown our chance and will be rejected by God.

God is not an angry, abusive master who is ready to punish us at every mistake. He is our loving Father! While *He will by no means clear the guilty*

(*Exodus* 34.7); those who open their hearts to Him will never be rejected! *No eye has seen a God besides you, who acts for those who wait for him. You meet him who joyfully works righteousness, those who remember you in your ways...*, Isaiah 64.4b-5.

Praise God for His matchless grace!

For Thought and Reflection:

1. What is a simple definition of grace?

2. What are three things God gives us that we do not deserve?

3. In what way did God "bear the cost" for us?

4. Why is it often tempting to use God's grace as a crutch to not work in strengthening our weaknesses?

5. In what condition were we when God gave the gift of His son?

6. What is the difference between "cheap" and "free" grace?

7. What happens when we serve God from the perspective of slave/ master?

8. What happens when we serve God from the perspective of child/ father?

9. How do we live in God's grace?

10. Today's lesson has helped my assurance of salvation by:

Justified in Christ

Introduction:

The mood in the courtroom was tense. The families of both the victim and the guilty party were crammed into the room, along with many of their friends and supporters. A media circus had formed outside the courthouse. This only fueled the tension in the atmosphere. A few months before, a vicious crime gripped the small town. The perpetrator was well known in the community. Many struggled with how something so awful could have ever happened when everything on the outside suggested a loving, caring, and happy family. For the victim's family, so devastated by what happened, almost **any** sentence handed down by the judge would not be enough. On the other side, the killer's family was filled with disbelief, embarrassment, remorse, and shock. While they wanted the judge to exercise compassion, they also understood the full gravity of the consequences the crime brought with it. For forty-five long minutes, everyone waited, talking in soft and whispered tones.

Suddenly and without warning, deputies escorted the guilty party into the room. A hush fell over the room. Finally, the judge appeared and after emotional testimony from witnesses on both sides, the judge delivered less than a life sentence. While the felon would be incarcerated many years, his total time served would be mitigated by good behavior and automatic reductions due to prison overcrowding. A few in the audience were relieved. The majority, however, were even more angry because they believed justice had not been served. For them, the punishment would never be great enough to erase the devastation of the crime.

Similar situations play out every day inside thousands of courtrooms across our country. Most Americans share a common viewpoint on justice. That is, we tend to believe justice is only served if the guilty party *gets what they deserve.* If, for some reason, this does not happen, we tend to believe justice is thwarted and the law made a mockery.

How does our American viewpoint of justice impact our thinking on biblical justification?

While biblical justice most certainly involves punishment of wrongdoing, in God's perspective, **justice always centers on fairness**. God's fairness is seen in everything. We can trust that He gives no advantage to those we consider successful, powerful, or important. **Every person** has equal access to God. The humble person whose heart is constantly ready to repent can be certain God will keep His promise to forgive.

Understanding Justification

Justification means to be "acquitted of guilt; to be declared righteous; to be found not guilty." The word is found only three times in the English Bible—every instance in Romans. *Justified* is found thirty-four times. It means to be freed from sin and reconciled to God. In Christianity, justification is accomplished through Jesus Christ. *But the words "it was counted to him" were not written for his sake alone, but for ours also. It will be counted to us who believe in him who raised from the dead Jesus our Lord, who was delivered up for our trespasses and raised for our justification,* Romans 4.23-25.

Every human sins, Romans 3.23; 5.12; 2 Chronicles 6.36. In His law, God has decreed that sin brings with it the penalty of death, Ezekiel 18.20; Romans 2.6-9; 6.23. While salvation is by grace, it is not by grace alone. While salvation is made possible through God's mercy, it is not by mercy alone. Our salvation is also an act of divine justice. Grace, love, and mercy never overpower law. Mercy does not overwhelm God's wrath. Compassion does not conquer God's justice. All these things work together in perfect harmony. Romans 3.21-31 presents salvation as the perfect action of divine justice coupled with God's grace. In saving us, justice was not ignored. It was met and fully satisfied.

God is a God of justice. Consider these three Old Testament passages:

- **Numbers 14.18** — *The LORD is slow to anger and abounding in steadfast love, forgiving iniquity and transgression, but he will by no means clear the* *guilty, visiting the iniquity of the fathers on the children, to the third and the fourth generation.*

- **Proverbs 11.21** — *Be assured, an evil person will not go unpunished, but the offspring of the righteous will be delivered.*

- **Nahum 1.3** — *The LORD is slow to anger and great in power, and the LORD will by no means clear the guilty. His way is in whirlwind and storm, and the clouds are the dust of his feet.*

Even hidden or unknown sins will be accounted for. You see, God's justice demands payment. Every sin will be accounted for.

> No sin ever committed by anyone, anytime, known, or unknown, will go unpunished. God's mercy is not some sentimentality that softens His justice. Absolute justice must be satisfied, and it will be satisfied.[11]

Yet, while every sin will be accounted for, mercy will be given to help the guilty. God is both a just God **and** a Savior, Isaiah 45.21. Justification and acquittal come through Jesus to all by virtue of **faith**. Justification is not found by law keeping. Those who live by faith are justified: *We know that a person is not justified by works of the law but through faith in Jesus Christ, so we also have believed in Christ Jesus, in order to be justified by faith in Christ and not by works of the law, because by works of the law no one will be justified,* Galatians 2.16. While the Mosaical covenant is under view in this passage, there is a higher principle in play. No person is ever justified by works of **any** law, **Old or New.** We will discuss this further in a later chapter.

When we believe in God through Jesus and demonstrate that belief through a living and active faith, God pronounces us to be justified based on the sinless life and sacrifice of Jesus. There are three passages that explicitly state this fact:

- **Romans 3.24-26** — We are *justified by his grace as a gift, through the redemption that is in Christ Jesus, whom God put forward as a propitiation by his blood, to be received by faith. This was to show God's righteousness, because in his divine forbearance he had passed over former sins. It was to* *show his righteousness at the present time, so that he might be just and the justifier of the one who has faith in Jesus.*

- **1 Peter 2.24** — *He himself bore our sins in his body on the tree, that we might die to sin and live to righteousness. By his wounds you have been healed.*

- **2 Corinthians 5.20-21** — *Therefore, we are ambassadors for Christ, God making his appeal through us. We implore you on behalf of Christ, be reconciled to God. For our sake he made him to be sin who knew no sin, so that in him we might become the righteousness of God.*

Justification happens when the sinner is cleansed of sin and pronounced righteous by God. This happens through our repentance, confession, and immersion in the waters of baptism. *In Him also you were circumcised with a circumcision made without hands, by putting off the body of the flesh, by the circumcision of Christ, having been buried with Him in baptism, in which you were also raised with Him through faith in the powerful working of God, who raised Him from the dead,* Colossians 2.11-12. We are justified in our initial obedience to Christ and remain justified so long as we continue to walk in the light of fellowship with Jesus.

Walking in the Light

Continued devotion and faithfulness to God is absolutely required. Our salvation and subsequent sanctification is not just an event—it is a process. The meaning of walking in the light is found in 1 John 1.6-9. Observe the parallels presented between verses 6-7 and 8-9:

1.6-7	1.8-9
If we say we have fellowship with Him while we walk in darkness, we lie ...	*If we say we have no sin, we deceive ourselves ...*
and we do not practice the truth ...	*and the truth is not in us ...*
But, if we walk in the light as He is in the light ...	*If we confess our sins ...*
we have fellowship with one another ...	*He is faithful and just to forgive us our sins...*
and the blood of Jesus His Son cleanses us from all sin.	*and to cleanse us from all unrighteousness.*

Looking at the parallels negatively, we see that denying our sin is part of what it means to walk in darkness. Deemphasizing our sinfulness cuts off fellowship with God. Those who walk in darkness seek to conceal and lessen the seriousness of sin. Looking positively, 1 John 1.6-9 stresses the fact that God's sons and daughters confess their sin **as a regular pattern of life**. **Walking in the light does not mean perfection**. Christians sin. The struggle with sin will not end until the cessation of our physical life. If walking in the light means perfection, there would be no need for the final phrase of 1.7 - *the blood of Jesus His Son cleanses us from all sin*. 1.8 also gives us a strong warning against claiming to be sinless while we walk in the light.

Walking in the light is more than sincerity or good intentions. It is the very definition of Christian living. *Walk in a manner worthy of the calling to which you have been called*, Ephesians 4.1. This involves a lifestyle where one commits to becoming like God—working each day to put on His character. It is dedication to leading a life of holiness and purity. *Whoever keeps his commandments abides in God, and God in him. And by this we know that he abides in us, by the Spirit whom he has given us*, 1 John 3.24.

Walking in the light involves walking in truth. This implies that we must embrace God's truth and oppose spiritual error, 1 John 2.21-23; 4.1, 6. When we *walk in the light,* we exercise our commitment to avoid a lifestyle of sin. That is, we resist becoming a defiant, persistent sinner who rejects repentance and confession. God's sons and daughters humbly serve God and do their best to steer clear of habitual and deliberate sin. "There is a world of difference between one sin committed by a sincere believer in his struggle against sin and the habit of sin."[12] *No one born of God **makes a practice of sinning**, for God's seed abides in him, and he cannot keep on sinning because he has been born of God*, 1 John 3.9 [emphasis mine]. When we steer clear of the **practice** of sin, we walk in the light.

Walking in the light involves a new attitude toward sin. We must not treat sin lightly. When we sin, we know we can confess it to God and be forgiven. But, **we must not abuse God's cleansing. Sin is something**

we can avoid. In fact, Scripture instructs us to conquer our sins—to rise above them through the strength of God. *Let not sin therefore reign in your mortal body, to make you obey its passions. Do not present your members to sin as instruments for unrighteousness, but **present yourselves to God as those who have been brought from death to life**, and your members to God as instruments for righteousness. For sin will have no dominion over you, since you are not under law but under grace*, Romans 6.12-14 [emphasis mine]. We have the choice as to who we will obey. Will we make the conscious decision to remain justified by continuing to walk in the light? *Do you not know that if you present yourselves to anyone as obedient slaves, you are slaves of the one whom you obey, either of sin, which leads to death, or of obedience, which leads to righteousness?* Romans 6.16. **We don't have to sin.** As we grow in Christ, there should be a decreasing frequency of sin in our lives. There is a popular idea in our religious world that says it is not important to pay attention to our sin. If we engage in sin, **we can't just ignore it.** We must acknowledge it for what it is, and seek the forgiveness of God.

How Do We Remain Justified while Struggling with Sin?

But if we walk in the light, as he is in the light, we have fellowship with one another, and the blood of Jesus his Son cleanses us from all sin. If we confess our sins, he is faithful and just to forgive us our sins and to cleanse us from all unrighteousness, 1 John 1.7, 9.

Verse 7 emphasizes God's **promise**. It is declared in the word *cleanses*. In the original language, the word is written in present tense.

> Any controversy from this passage should not revolve around whether or not the cleansing is *continual* (because the word clearly suggests continuous action, i.e, the blood of Jesus **keeps on cleansing**), but whether or not continual cleansing is *conditional*. [emphasis mine][13]

Not only does *cleanses* denote continual action, but also the problem of sin is presented as a present tense problem. *If we say we **have no sin**, we deceive* *ourselves, and the truth is not in us,* 1.8 [emphasis mine]. So how do we deal with the ever-present problem of sin? What is the cleansing conditioned upon?

Verse 9 emphasizes the Christian's **responsibility and behavior**. It is declared in the word *confess.* Just like the wording in the previous two verses, *confess* is written in present tense. 1.9 clearly teaches that our role in this matter is to confess our sin. Confession is not some formality, ceremony, or procedure. Rather, it involves an **attitude** where we continually engage in the process.

> One's attitude of heart toward God is regret at ever offending God and a constant changing of the mind about sin (repentance). That is accompanied by confessing our sins and relying on the blood of Christ for cleansing. **Our cleansing is always conditional.** [emphasis mine][14]

Look closely at the end of 1.9. God promises to cleanse us of **all** sin. **Our salvation is not dependent upon our perfection—but on God's cleansing**! No person can be sinlessly perfect, but **every person can be responsible**. 1 John 1.7-9 is a source of extreme encouragement for the Christian who walks in the light.

How many grow discouraged because of constant failures? Do you ever feel embarrassed to approach God over and over to confess and ask for forgiveness because of personal weakness and vulnerability to sin? The blood of Jesus will cleanse you from **all** sin—not some, not most … but **all** sin! *We can never come too often to God when we come in humble penitence and faith.*[15] God wants to forgive people who want forgiveness. He forgives people who realize they need forgiveness. He forgives people who feel truly unworthy of forgiveness.

For the person who keeps his or her heart aligned with God, God finds it a joy to forgive. It is in His very nature. Our sins *are forgiven for His name's sake,* 1 John 2.12. It is about us walking hand in hand with God. We no longer hold on to our sin; we get it out in the open so God can cleanse us completely.

Notice 1.9 again. Those who are forgiven are the ones whose lives are characterized by confession. Confession is something that rises up out of our hatred of sin. Just as God hates evil and iniquity, so must we. Whoever has been transformed develops the same attitude as God toward sin. How did Paul regard his life in the flesh? *Wretched man that I am! Who will deliver me from this body of death?* Romans 7.24. The ever-revealing light of God made Paul more than aware of the sin in his life. The same is true for us. As light penetrates our heart, we will mourn for our sin, Matthew 5.4. But, as we go on admitting our sin and confessing, the Lord goes on cleansing.

Continual confession characterizes Christians.[16]

Conclusion:

It is not about the messes you have made in your life, it is about living responsibly now. We remain justified in God's sight as long as we direct our lives away from our past and move toward God. When we repent and confess our sins, we make the commitment to refuse to allow our past determine who we are. We commit our trust to the power of God to cleanse and forgive us of all sin.

Christians have been acquitted of all guilt and declared righteous. God has pronounced us not guilty. We have been reconciled to Him. We have been justified and will remain so as long as we are committed to serving Him—walking in the light, confessing our sins and shortcomings. Those who live in the kingdom are no longer under the threat of eternal condemnation! *There is therefore now no condemnation for those who are in Christ Jesus. Those who live according to the flesh* (walk in darkness) *set their minds on the things of the flesh, but those who live according to the Spirit* (walk in the light) *set their minds on the things of the Spirit,* Romans 8.1, 5. You can live with hope and optimism, looking forward to heaven—knowing it is God's gift to you.

For Thought and Reflection:

1. Describe your perception of American justice. How does that affect our perspective on justice in Christianity?

2. Justification means:

3. Justification and acquittal come through Jesus to all men by virtue of:

4. At what point are we initially justified (acquitted)?

5. What does it mean to walk in the light?

6. What is a *lifestyle of sin?*

7. In 1 John 1:7, what does God promise to do for the Christian?

8. In 1 John 1:9, what is the Christian responsible for?

9. Is our salvation dependent upon our perfection? Why/Why not?

10. What can you do today to build a deeper trust in God's ability to forgive you of your sin?

Jesus: The Offering That
Turned Away God's Wrath

Introduction:

Where were you when you first heard about the events of September 11, 2001? Just as the John F. Kennedy assassination riveted a nation thirty-eight years before, the terrorists' attacks on that beautiful September morning jolted many Americans with the reality of radical Islam's intense desire to destroy the West. Think back to your thoughts as you watched the towers fall to the ground. What went through your mind when you received word that the Pentagon had been attacked? How did you feel when you heard about the plane crash in Pennsylvania? Remember the silence as you looked across the brilliantly clear sky and saw no air traffic... anywhere! Were you angry as you watched cable television report on the reaction of our enemies in the Middle East? If you are like me, one of your first reactions was that the enemy needed to pay, and pay dearly. Justice demanded it. Almost 3,000 Americans died that day in innocent blood. The lives of their families, their loved ones, and a nation would be forever changed.

More recently, our country endured a week of sadness and trepidation during the Boston Marathon bombings. How could anyone be so vicious as to callously plant a bomb feet away from innocent people? What moves a person to shoot a police officer in cold blood? How did you feel on the Thursday evening and throughout the day on Friday as authorities launched the largest manhunt in American history? Were you ready for justice to be done?

The need to deal out justice gives us a very small taste of how it must be for God. When sin is committed, God's justice demands punishment. In fact, every violation of God's law is subject to His punishment. This involves every thought, motive, and the deepest of secrets. There will be a day when *God judges the secrets of men by Christ Jesus*, Romans 2.16. Every person who has ever lived will give an account to God: *For we must all appear before the judgment seat of Christ, so that each one may receive what is due for what he has done in the body, whether good or evil*, 2 Corinthians 5.10.

On the last, great day, God will pour out His wrath on those who stand before Him unprepared. When we think of wrath, we might imagine a burning anger, a fiery rage, and God's extreme hatred of sin and indignation of evil. God's wrath was clearly demonstrated throughout the Old Testament, where there are over 375 references to punishment for rebellion and sin against God. *The LORD is a jealous and avenging God; the LORD is avenging and wrathful; the LORD takes vengeance on his adversaries and keeps wrath for his enemies. The LORD is slow to anger and great in power, and the LORD will by no means clear the guilty. His way is in whirlwind and storm, and the clouds are the dust of his feet*, Nahum 1.2–3.

Many of the same words and connotations are carried over in the New Testament. For example: *It is a fearful thing to fall into the hands of the living God*, Hebrews 10.31. No matter which dispensation, we must realize that God will move with the severest wrath to punish sin. He will hide His face from those who rebel against Him. It is this wrath and punishment from which we have been rescued. *He will render to each one according to his works: to those who by patience in well-doing seek for glory and honor and immortality, he will give eternal life; but for those who are self-seeking and do not obey the truth, but obey unrighteousness, there will be wrath and fury*, Romans 2.6–8.

God's Love and Justice: Both Satisfied on the Cross

You may have heard someone claim there are two gods in the Bible. The God of the Old Testament is usually depicted as a God of fire, punishment, and vengeance. In contrast, the God of the New Testament is seen as loving, gracious, and filled with mercy. And for the casual observer, this may seem true. With the exception of eight souls, God destroyed human life in a worldwide flood, Genesis 6–7. God punished Sodom and Gomorrah with fire and brimstone, Genesis 19. He smote the men and women of the Midianites, Numbers 31. He utterly destroyed the Amalekites, 1 Samuel 15. There are many other examples. And again, a superficial look at the New Testament reveals a God of love, culminating in God's ultimate gift, the giving of His Son on a cross to redeem the world from sin.

So, is this an accurate perception? Not really. Old Testament Bible characters knew a great deal about God's forgiveness.

- **Micah 7.18** — *Who is a God like you, pardoning iniquity and passing over transgression for the remnant of his inheritance? He does not retain his anger forever, because he delights in steadfast love.*

- **Psalm 103.12** — *as far as the east is from the west, so far does he remove our transgressions from us.*

- **Psalm 51.1–2** — *Have mercy on me, O God, according to your steadfast love; according to your abundant mercy blot out my transgressions. Wash me thoroughly from my iniquity, and cleanse me from my sin!*

And, who could forget the story of Jonah? Commissioned by God to go to Nineveh and call out for their repentance, Jonah balked. The Assyrians were the greatest national threat to Israel. Jonah would have been glad to go and pronounce judgment on them, but entreat them to repent? He understood that if they did, **God would forgive them.** We know the story. After an eventful ship ride to Tarshish, and an attention getting experience inside the belly of a great fish, Jonah went to Nineveh. They repented, and God did not destroy them. Jonah 4 records the prophet's reaction. He had a very hard time understanding how God could demonstrate justice by forgiving such wicked and godless people.

In fact, there were many of God's servants during Old Testament times who wondered about God's justice—especially when sinners flourished, lived, and even prospered. Some of God's servants charged God with being tolerant of sin and became very critical. For example, observe:

- **Psalm 78.38** — *Yet he, being compassionate, atoned for their iniquity and did not destroy them; he restrained his anger often and did not stir up all his wrath.*

- **Malachi 2.17** — *You have wearied the Lord with your words. But you say, "How have we wearied him?" By saying, "Everyone who does evil is good in the sight of the Lord, and he delights in them." Or by asking, "Where is the God of justice?"*

- **Malachi 3.14–16** — *You have said, 'It is vain to serve God. What is the profit of our keeping his charge or of walking as in mourning before the Lord of hosts? And now we call the arrogant blessed. Evildoers not only prosper but they put God to the test and they escape.' Then those who feared the Lord spoke with one another. The Lord paid attention and heard them, and a book of remembrance was written before him of those who feared the Lord and esteemed his name.*

When we begin to probe into the pages of the New Testament, it is also very easy to find a loving, compassionate, and forgiving God.

So, is our God a God of cheap forgiveness? How can God be so forgiving? Perhaps this is the question Paul had in his mind as he penned Romans 3.21–31. Paul started out the section by stating that righteousness is obtained *apart from law.* Righteousness comes *by faith.* Some may have wondered how God can be righteous and still justify the one who has faith in Jesus? In their mind, they may ask, "Where are the wages of sin?"

Romans 3.25–26 answers these questions. God's love and justice come together at the cross. We are redeemed through Christ Jesus *whom God put forward as a propitiation by his blood, to be received by faith. This was to show God's righteousness, because in his divine forbearance he had passed over former sins. It was to show his righteousness at the present time, so that he might be just and the justifier of the one who has faith in Jesus.* What do we learn here? **God's justice was satisfied when Jesus died.** This included people who lived before and after the cross. God forgives men and women of their sin **because Jesus paid the penalty on the cross**, Isaiah 53.4–6; 1 Peter 2.21–

25. Because of His great love, God gave us His Son, John 3.16; Romans 5.6–10; 1 John 4.9–10.

Since this is the case, Paul says that salvation is not by a law of works, Romans 3.27. It is *by the law of faith*. Everything was designed by God and achieved through Jesus. The cross is all grace and we accept God's gift of love in faith. Because of this, there is no room for boasting. All the glory goes to God. **Salvation is not about human achievement**. When we understand the work of Jesus on the cross, we will move away from trusting in our goodness and acts of service. We sometimes sing:

> In Christ alone my hope is found, He is my light, my strength, my song; this Cornerstone, this Solid Ground, firm through the fiercest drought and storm. What heights of love, what depths of peace, when fears are stilled, when strivings cease! My Comforter, my all in all; here in the love of Christ I stand.

> In Christ alone, who took on flesh, fullness of God in helpless Babe; this gift of love and righteousness scorned by the ones He came to save. 'Til on that cross as Jesus died, the wrath of God was satisfied, for every sin on Him was laid; here in the death of Christ I live.

> There in the ground His body lay, Light of the world by darkness slain; then bursting forth in glorious day, up from the grave He rose again. And as He stands in victory, sin's curse has lost its grip on me, for I am His and He is mine; bought with the precious blood of Christ.

> No guilt in life, no fear in death, this is the pow'r of Christ in me; from life's first cry to final breath, Jesus commands my destiny. No pow'r of hell, no scheme of man, can ever pluck me from His hand, 'till He returns or calls me home; here in the power of Christ I'll stand.[17]

Since salvation is by faith, we might ask, "What kind of faith?" The faith in view in Romans 3.27 is:

- **Rooted in a love for God**, Matthew 22.37-40

- **Seen in ongoing repentance and confession of sin**, 1 John 1.7–9

- **Witnessed by self-denial**, Matt 16.24–26

- **Demonstrated obedience and love for God's word**, 2 Tim 3.16–17

Jesus: Propitiation for Our Sin

Propitiation is a "Bible word." It is hardly used in our regular vernacular. While only seen four times in the New Testament (Romans 3.25; 1 John 2.2, 4.10; Hebrews 2.17), it lies at the very foundation of Christianity. *Propitiation* has a Latin origin and was used to describe the pious efforts of the heathen in obtaining the favor of the gods.

> The background of the related Greek terms is interesting. These words were used of a sacrifice one brought in order to appease the anger of the gods. The individual chanced that the attitude of the god or gods might be altered, hoping that the gods would be disposed to look upon the person with favor, from which further blessings might follow.[18]

Unlike pagan deities who are said to have delighted in persecuting their subjects and reveled in taking revenge, our God acted on His own and provided the sacrificial offering that covers our sin and makes reconciliation possible.

> *But if anyone does sin, we have an advocate with the Father, Jesus Christ the righteous. He is the propitiation for our sins, and not for ours only but also for the sins of the whole world.*
>
> — 1 John 2.1*b*–2

In the New Testament, *propitiation* is connected with our initial salvation and remains a part of our day to day life as a Christian. When we became part of God's family we were delivered (rescued) from God's wrath, Colossians 1.13; 2.11–14. In the Bible, *propitiation is an offering that turns away God's wrath.* Because Jesus willingly allowed the anger of God to be diverted to Him, those who believe in Him have salvation, Romans 3.25–26. Jesus covered what was offensive (sin) as to restore our broken fellowship with the Father. *He himself bore our sins in his body on the tree, that we might die to sin and live to righteousness,* 1 Peter 2.24.

An excellent foreshadowing of what Jesus did for us is seen in Exodus 12. There, the children of Israel were told to kill a young lamb, one year old, without spot or blemish. Its blood was to be painted on the doorposts and on the lintel of their house. Because they followed His instructions, God passed over their homes and did not strike down the first-born. Ultimately, Jesus is the fulfillment of the Passover. He was the sacrificial lamb, offered up in perfection, without sin, spot, or blemish. Those who are washed in His blood (baptism) are covered and will be spared from eternal death.

Both the Father and Son participated willingly in this process. The offering of Jesus was more than enough to cover the sins of everyone who will ever live on earth.

> *But we see him who for a little while was made lower than the angels, namely Jesus, crowned with glory and honor because of the suffering of death, so that by the grace of God he might taste death for everyone. For it was fitting that he, for whom and by whom all things exist, in bringing many sons to glory, should make the founder of their salvation perfect through suffering. For he who sanctifies and those who are sanctified all have one source. ...*
>
> — Hebrews 2.9–11

Jesus stood in our place. He bore the brunt of God's wrath and paid the price for our sin. *We implore you on behalf of Christ, be reconciled to God. For our sake he made him to be sin who knew no sin, so that in him we might become the righteousness of God,* 2 Corinthians 5.20–21. Your sin, my sin, and the sin of everyone who has or will live was placed upon His shoulders. **Jesus is the offering that turns away the wrath of God**.

Propitiation Was Not Made So We Can Choose to Walk in Darkness

So now, let's think about the Christian life post initial salvation. What about the Christian who engages in premeditated sin? What about the

Christian who continually succumbs to Satan's devices and regularly chooses to turn his or her heart away from seeking God? What I am describing is a situation where a Christian knows the will of God, understands the consequences, and still chooses to act on the temptation. Can this person count on the cleansing of God?

The simple answer is: "**No, not until the behavior is confessed before God and repented of.**" When we deliberately choose to sin, we are rejecting the need to see sin the way God sees it and respond to it in the way He does. If a person chooses to engage in acts of darkness, there is no reason to believe that his or her sins are covered. **There is no assurance of salvation while you are living in disobedience.** *Why do you call me 'Lord, Lord,' and not do what I tell you? Luke 6.46. Do not be deceived: God is not mocked, for whatever one sows, that will he also reap. For the one who sows to his own flesh will from the flesh reap corruption, but the one who sows to the Spirit will from the Spirit reap eternal life, Galatians 6.7-8.* We need to possess a sense of urgency in how we approach God and our sin. **Every action we engage in carries with it the weight of eternity.** This knowledge should lead us to real faith that changes and saves us.

> Truth is a razor's edge between two errors. One error is to think that conduct after conversion has nothing to do with salvation. The other error is to believe that our conduct after conversion must be perfect.[19]

When we appeal to Christ for salvation, we must allow truth to take up residence in our heart. When we open our heart, God's light will shine inside. **His light does not immediately drive out all falsehood and sin.** It is a battle that lasts a lifetime. When truth comes in, it reveals sin. **The mark of a Christian is not sinlessness, but sin consciousness**. The mark of spiritual maturity is deep and abiding brokenness for sin. A new life in Christ is not a superficial positive self-concept. **It is confidence in the abounding grace of God through Jesus Christ.**

Propitiation Is Continually Made for Those Who Walk in the Light

Many Christians do their very best to live a holy life, but still struggle with sin. Temptation and the war with Satan do not vanish after salvation. **When we sin, we are still a child of God.** Our relationship with God will continue as long as we acknowledge our sin and shortcomings. When we realize we've sinned and seek God's forgiveness, Jesus stands on our side because He is our *Advocate*. He is well acquainted with the shortcomings of the human condition and testifies on our behalf. Consider these passages:

- **Hebrews 2.11–14** — *For he who sanctifies and those who are sanctified all have one source. That is why he is not ashamed to call them brothers, saying, "I will tell of your name to my brothers; in the midst of the congregation I will sing your praise." And again, "I will put my trust in him." And again, "Behold, I and the children God has given me." Since therefore the children share in flesh and blood, he himself likewise partook of the same things, that through death he might destroy the one who has the power of death, that is, the devil.*

- **Hebrews 7.25** — *Consequently, he is able to save to the uttermost those who draw near to God through him, since he always lives to make intercession for them.*

- **1 John 2.1–2** — *My little children, I am writing these things to you so that you may not sin. But if anyone does sin, we have an advocate with the Father, Jesus Christ the righteous. He is the propitiation for our sins, and not for ours only but also for the sins of the whole world.*

The 1 John passage is especially important because in the background a courtroom scene is in view. Jesus stands up and argues that He met God's demand for justice (through His death) and defeats our accuser (Satan). Our Lord has never lost a case. He always obtains forgiveness for those who yield their heart to Him.

The New Testament writers labored very hard to demonstrate Jesus as the righteous One who wants to help.

(He delivered) *all those who through fear of death were subject to lifelong slavery. For surely it is not angels that he helps, but he helps the offspring of Abraham. Therefore he had to be made like his brothers in every respect, so that he might become a merciful and faithful high priest in the service of God, to make propitiation for the sins of the people. For because he himself has suffered when tempted, he is able to help those who are being tempted.*

— Hebrews 2.14–18

Conclusion:

God is on our side! When we come to Him in prayer, seeking His forgiveness, we are forgiven! When we walk in obedience, Jesus **continues** to be the propitiation for our sin each and every day.

Are you living with this assurance? Praise God for His great love and the willingness of deity in offering itself on our behalf so we can have eternal salvation!

For Thought and Reflection:

1. How do the events of September 11, 2001, or the 2013 Boston bombing better help you to understand God's need to execute justice upon those who do evil?

2. What matters in our lives will be under consideration on judgment day?

3. What was God's purpose in sending Jesus?

4. What is the background on the word "propitiation"?

5. How is propitiation inseparably connected with salvation?

6. What is a short definition of propitiation?

7. How does Exodus 12 relate to today's lesson?

8. What most impresses you about 2 Corinthians 5.20-21?

9. How does Jesus continue to serve as propitiation for Christians today?

10. Today's lesson has helped my assurance of salvation by:

Living by Trust in Jesus, Not Ourselves

Introduction:

For by grace you have been saved through faith. And this is not your own doing;
it is the gift of God, not a result of works, so that no one may boast.
For we are his workmanship, created in Christ Jesus for good works,
which God prepared beforehand, that we should walk in them.

— Ephesians 2.8–10

In American religion, properly defining *salvation by grace through faith* is a serious challenge. While the concept is clearly taught in Scripture, an informal survey might reveal many varying definitions. Man-made doctrines have led some individuals to reach very different conclusions from what has been divinely revealed. Part of the problem results from how some define *faith*.

What has the Holy Spirit revealed? A proper understanding of the meaning of *faith* in Ephesians 2.8 will go far in clearing up the confusion that encompasses our world. Is the faith here only a mental acknowledgement of the Lordship of Jesus? Or is more involved? The faith mentioned Ephesians 2.8 is defined in Hebrews 11.1, 6: *Now faith is the assurance of things hoped for, the conviction of things not seen. And without faith it is impossible to please him, for whoever would draw near to God must believe that he exists and that he rewards those who seek him.* These two verses are a presentation of the biblical definition and essentialness of faith. In the original language, *faith* implies an emphasis on trust in God's power and His nearness to help. There is much more to *faith* than belief that God exists and that His word is true. ***Faith* involves our conviction to act** in response to God's expectations, **in humility and total dependence on the power of God for providing the blessing**.

This is the meaning of faith in Ephesians 2.8: a *faith that works*. It involves a full surrender to Christ and this *genuine faith* with always be accompanied by the evidence of obedience, James 2.14–26. If a person claims to believe but does not obey, he or she will not be saved, Luke 6.46.

> We work from grace, not for it. Our work is the response to God's work in us.[20]

In Matthew 9.20–22, a woman with a discharge of blood was healed by touching the fringe of Jesus' garment. She was told, *your faith has made you well,* 9.22. Was Jesus referring to her mental assent that He was the Messiah? Or, was He speaking of her deep conviction and trust in His ability to heal? She acted with full conviction that only He could provide her with the help she needed. **It is the active faith that saves**. The Hebrew writer says God *rewards those who seek Him,* 11.6. What are we seeking from Him? Salvation! He is the only one who can provide what we desperately need! Salvation rests in our *faith* in His power to save—not in ourselves. God, not our own works, is the object of our faith!

Salvation Is Not a Matter of Pay-As-You-Go

Learning not to depend on ourselves in our religious pursuit is very difficult. Culturally, Americans are rooted in a strong work ethic. For generations, the *American Dream* stressed healthy rewards in exchange for hard work. Just about all of us are familiar with the concept of how *hard work pays off.* So, many are very comfortable with a religious concept that places trust in rewards that will be received because of pleasing acts or deeds performed. For many, the realization of the inability of any Christian to earn his or her salvation creates a strong sense of discomfort. "The understanding that no human act in response to God, not even a martyr's death, can place God in debt is distressing. Most Christians intensely dislike having to be at the 'mercy of grace.'"[21]

There are a number of Christians who view salvation as something similar to an item being placed on a "pay-as-you-go plan." In other words, this is the idea that we "earn our salvation" over time through the continuation of good works. All the while, God constantly scrutinizes our works, giving us salvation as we keep "making payments" through meticulous and precise following of commands, examples, and inferences. If we err in any way or do not have enough good works, our soul could be lost. Usually passages like Matthew 7.21–23 are added for emphasis. **This understanding makes salvation precarious at best. It leads to constant anxiety and doubt.**

How many works are enough?

What if a command was not performed exactly right?

What if something has been left undone?

The idea of earned salvation is not found in Scripture. It is an invention of man. Our salvation was paid for, **in full**, on the cross of Calvary by Jesus, Romans 3.25-26. Salvation is provided by Christ through His work as a free gift, Romans 6.23b. Our trust is placed in Jesus, not our works. We simply cannot work our way into heaven. *For by works of the law no human being will be justified in His sight, … then what becomes of our boasting? It is excluded. By what kind of law? By a law of works? No, but by the law of faith,* Romans 3.20, 27. God has never saved any person by works….**of any law.**

Still, many Christians seek to "work" their way to heaven—trying to prove their worthiness and secure their spot the best way they know how. How do you view obedience? Is it an expression of your appreciation for what you have already received in Christ? Is it born out of your active trust in God? Is it the fruit of a productive relationship with the Savior? Or, do you trust your obedience more than your faith, believing you are made righteous because of the good deeds you do?

No relationship with God <u>is produced</u> through any form of obedient behavior. Deeds alone are insufficient. Even when we have done all we can do, we are still *unworthy servants, having done only what was our duty,* Luke 17.10. Christians are made righteous by their faith, Romans 5.1.

> The Christian's obedience is his response to what God has done for him and for all men in Jesus Christ. Its basic motive is gratitude for God's goodness in Christ. This means that all truly Christian moral endeavors

are theocentric, having their origin not in a humanistic desire for the enhancement of the self by the attainment of a moral superiority, nor in the legalist's illusory hope of putting God under an obligation to himself, but simply in the gracious action of God.[22]

This is not the *faith only* teaching so popular in our day. This is not the *easy belief, no commitment* type of religion taught by preachers and teachers on cable networks and internet blogs. Rather, total dependence on God requires the highest type of commitment. It requires the sacrifice of what is most important to us: **ourselves**.

> ... *'If anyone would come after me, let him deny himself and take up his cross and follow me. For whoever would save his life will lose it, but whoever loses his life for my sake will find it. For what will it profit a man if he gains the whole world and forfeits his soul? Or what shall a man give in return for his soul?'*
>
> — Matthew 16.24–26

Some people know how to **do** many deeds, but have never given **themselves** to God. Are these the ones spoken to in Matthew 7.21–23? Our response to God is much, much more than just doing. It is the active engagement of our heart, doing acts through faith.

In our rightful resistance to the doctrine of salvation by faith alone, we must not move to the opposite extreme. While most New Testament Christians rightly deny Old Testament law keeping as a basis for salvation, some have turned the New Testament into a book of law and use works as the basis for salvation. This is a recipe for spiritual failure. Do not afflict yourself with a losing battle to earn your salvation. Never subject yourself to anguish, trying to gain acceptance to God on the basis of your good works.

Salvation Is by Faith—Romans 3–4

In these two chapters, Paul clearly teaches that righteousness (salvation) comes by faith. What the *works* are in Romans 3.27-5.1, has been the source of great dispute among Christians. Some believe it refers to works of the Old Testament law. And while what Paul says certainly fits with this idea, the context implies there is a larger principle involved. (See 4.13.) That is, we are saved by faith, not by the keeping of **any** law. Others believe the *works* here cover individual works of merit or tradition, or even *perfect law keeping.*

As you study this section of Romans, remember the overlying principle rests upon whether we will trust in what **we do** in obeying God, or trust **in what God has done.** Romans 3.21 and 5.1 essentially serve as bookends in a passage that uses Abraham to prove our salvation rests on the work of Christ.

Here, Paul teaches:

God's justice was fully satisfied by the death of Jesus on the cross, 3.21–30. All accountable individuals are in need of salvation. The righteousness of God has been manifested apart from law. This is the pinnacle of Paul's argument in the epistle to the Galatians: *...no one is justified before God by the law, for 'the righteous shall live by faith.' Christ redeemed us from the curse of the law by becoming a curse for us—for it is written, 'cursed is everyone who is hanged on a tree,'* Galatians 3.11, 13. *For freedom Christ has set us free; stand firm therefore, and do not submit again to a yoke of slavery,* Galatians 5.1. Going back to Romans 3, God is just in justifying sinners who appeal to Him through the blood of Christ. He is *the justifier of the one who has faith in Jesus,* 3.26.

God designed the cross to demonstrate His holiness, 3.31. Since salvation is by faith, does this mean God no longer cares about law keeping? *By no means!* By the new life we receive in salvation, we have been called to fulfill the law. Jesus did not come to destroy, but to *fulfill,* Matthew 5.17. We aren't saved to ignore God's law; we are saved to abide by it. God's people love His law, and long to obey it, because they have been saved by grace, Psalm 119.97. **Law was never designed to save. *It was designed to show you where you fall short.***

Abraham was *not* justified by works, 4.1-2. If so, he would have had the right to boast. Salvation has been designed to give glory to God, not glory to human beings.

Abraham was justified by faith, 4.3-8. Genesis 15.6 is quoted. Abraham lived long before the law of Moses. He was made righteous (right with God) through trust in God. **Abraham demonstrated trust through his actions.** Observing what is written regarding him in Hebrews 11 is especially helpful here. *By faith Abraham obeyed when he was called to go out to a place that he was to receive as an inheritance. And he went out, not knowing where he was going,* 11.8 [emphasis mine]. *He believed God.* He believed so much that he heeded God's call. Abraham's faith explained his actions. See also Hebrew 11.9 and 17. Abraham is always associated with faith. He moved with spiritual vision, patiently trusting God every step of the way.

How does this tie back in with Romans 4.3–8? The concept of salvation by grace through faith was established long before Israel received the law of Moses. God still justifies men and women on this basis today.

Abraham was justified by grace, not law, 4.9-17. I believe the key verse in this section is 4.13. The old law is not the only thing in view. In fact, in this verse the usage of the word *the* is not found in the original Greek text. It reads, *that he would be heir of the world did not come **through law** but through the righteousness of faith.* While certainly applicable, the old law is not the only thing in view. There is a higher principle in play. **Salvation is never based solely on law keeping.** *Is the law then contrary to the promises of God? Certainly not! For if a law had been given that could give life, then righteousness would indeed be by the law,* Galatians 3.21. Just as in Romans 4.13, the word *the* is left out of the original language. Salvation is by faith through grace. The righteousness Abraham enjoyed was not achieved by the principle of works. His favor with God was founded on the basis of grace. Why?

See 4.15. *For the law brings wrath …* It was Ezekiel who said, *The soul who sins shall die,* 18.20a. Its purpose is to show us our sin. *Yet if it had not been for the law, I would not have known sin. … For I would not have known what* it is to covet if the law had not said, 'You shall not covet,' Romans 7.7. Those who attempt to justify themselves by works of any law are under a curse, Galatians 3.10. The curse is that those who approach God this way are bound to *abide by all things written in the book of the law, to perform them.* Is a human being capable of perfection? What law of God has a human being ever kept perfectly? This is why salvation is by faith. *Now it is evident that no one is justified before God by the law, for 'The righteous shall live by faith,'* Galatians 3.11. Again, the article *the* has been added here. The higher principle always applies; salvation is never made possible by human law keeping.

Abraham was justified by divine power, not human effort, Romans 4.18-25. When we first become acquainted with *the father of faith,* he is known as Abram, Genesis 11.26. There was a great irony associated with the meaning of his name. Abram, "exalted father," had no children. During this time there was nothing more humiliating for a husband and wife than the inability to have children. His wife, Sarai, was barren, Genesis 11.30.

When God first appeared to Abram he promised that through him would come a great nation, Genesis 12.2. Abram was 75 years old, 12.4. Years later, God is still talking about offspring. *I will make your offspring as the dust of the earth, so that if one can count the dust of the earth, your offspring also can be counted,* Genesis 13.16. But there were no children yet. Think of what this must have been like. Abram became very rich in livestock, silver, and gold, 13.2. Located on a major trade-route between Egypt and the Middle East, any caravan coming through would have used his wells. People would buy food and supplies from Abram. In the evening, the merchants would come by Abram's tent to pay their respects. Can you imagine what went through Abram's mind each time he was asked his name? He would answer:

"Abram, father of many."

"And, how many children do you have?" someone might ask.

"None." He would reply.

Can you imagine this scene playing out day by day ... *For over a decade?*[23]

By the time we get to Genesis 15, Abram is around 85 years old. He has dwelt in Canaan for ten years, 16.3. God is still talking about offspring, and this time gets even more specific: *'your very own son shall be your heir. Look toward heaven, and number the stars, if you are able to number them.' Then he said to him, 'So shall your offspring be,'* 15.4b-5. To this we read, Abram *believed the Lord and He counted it to him as righteousness,* 15.6.

More time goes by and still no child has been produced. In sheer desperation, Sarai offers Abram her bond servant, Hagar, so an heir can be born. At the time, the decision made sense to both of them because it satisfied Abram's need for a descendant to pass his inheritance to. Abram was 86 years old.

Thirteen more years go by between Genesis 15 and 17. Now, at the age of 99, God appears to Abram and promises a son will be born to him by his wife, 17.15. Abram marveled. In fact, he laughed and said, *'Shall a child be born to a man who is a hundred years old? Shall Sarah, who is ninety years old, bear a child?'* Then he said, *'O that Ishmael might live before you!'* 17.17-18. God said Ishmael was not the one. By the power of God, Sarah would give birth to a son through which the inheritance would pass. From now on, Abram would be known as Abraham, "father of multitudes," 17.5. Abraham believed God and immediately circumcised himself, along with Ishmael, and all his servants, 17.22-27.

It is this story that Paul is referencing in the final section of Romans 4. Concerning the birth of Isaac, Abraham believed that God *gives life to the dead and calls into existence the things that do not exist. In hope he believed against hope, that he should become the father of many nations,* 4.17b-18a. Abraham had long passed the age of being able to bear a child, and Sarah was barren. But yet he hoped. For this to happen, he understood it was completely beyond human capability. This fact did not *weaken his faith when he considered his own body,* 4.19. In fact, he moved without doubt, possessing a faith that *grew strong as he gave glory to God,* **fully convinced that God was able to do what He had promised,** 4.20-21 [emphasis mine]. Notice 4.22-23. Paul makes the application. Because of Abraham's strong, active faith, it was *'counted to him as righteousness.'* Today, Christians are saved in the same way: on the basis of faith that Jesus is able to do what no human being can do—provide relief from the damning effect of sin. Remember, *salvation is not by works done by us in righteousness*, Titus 3.5. It is by the power of God.

Your faith in God's ability to save; your repentance; your confession; and your baptism were all acts of trust that God would wash away your sin by the blood of Christ. Consider the story of the lame beggar in Acts 3. *Lame from birth*, 3.2, the man spent his life laying on his backside—begging for alms. As Peter and John passed, he asked them for money. Instead, Peter commanded him to *rise up and walk!* 3.6. The lame man had to cooperate with that command. What if he did not believe? What if he refused Peter's assistance to help him up? The obvious fact is that he did believe. **Obedience is the expression of trust in God's power.** What happened when the man stood up? *And he took him by the right hand and raised him up, and immediately his feet and ankles were made strong*, 3.7. Where was the power in the lame man's healing? Was it bound up in his faithful response? No. **It was in God's power that healed him.** "This man did not strengthen his own legs by his faithful response. Only Jesus had that power."[24]

Conclusion:

Surrendering to God as a faith-based response is not asking God to save us because of our own righteousness. Salvation comes through God and His working; we simply surrender to His word and work. Praise God for His underserved, unearned, uninfluenced, and spontaneous mercy which is an expression of His great love.

For Thought and Reflection:

1. How can a proper understanding of the definition of faith help us to understand what is meant by *salvation by grace through faith?*

2. What is the biblical definition of faith? See Hebrews 11.1, 6.

3. In what way has American culture impacted our approach to religion?

4. What is the proper viewpoint on Christian obedience?

5. What is the overlapping principle behind Romans 3.21-5.1?

6. What should be our attitude toward law? See Romans 3.31; 7.12; Psalm 119.97.

7. Why was Abraham not justified by works?

8. What always accompanied Abraham's faith? Cite Scripture to prove your answer.

9. Why is salvation never based on law keeping?

10. What is the purpose of law?

11. By whose power did Abraham receive the son of promise?

12. What does Acts 3 teach us about the power behind our salvation? See also Titus 3.5.

13. Has this chapter challenged your perspective on how you were saved? In what way?

Walking in Newness of Life

Introduction:

The first eleven chapters of Romans are a wonderful discourse on God's great plan of redemption. All are under sin, Romans 1.18 –3.20, and without God's intervention, we are destined for eternal condemnation in hell. Beginning at Romans 3.21, Paul teaches how God stepped in and made salvation possible by grace through faith in Jesus' work on the cross. Romans 5 is a summary of the message of God's willingness to save. He offered full pardon and acquittal - despite our alignment against Him, 5.6-10. No matter how sinful we were, the power of God to save was far greater, reaching down to the lowest depth. He reunited us with Him inside a loving relationship. *Now the law came in to increase the trespass, but where sin increased, grace abounded all the more, so that, as sin reigned in death, grace also might reign through righteousness leading to eternal life through Jesus Christ our Lord,* Romans 5.20–21.

If Romans 3–5 deals with how we are saved, then chapters 6-8 are the next step inside a logical progression. What happened when we were saved? And, how do we live once we have been saved? There is an overarching principle in these chapters that expresses God's expectation for personal holiness among His people. After reading Paul's conclusions on how we are saved in chapter 5, some would have begun to question. *…Are we to continue in sin so that grace may abound?* 6.1. His emphatic answer comes with the strongest of language. *By no means!* We have *died to sin* and no longer *live in it,* 6.2b. Paul had already alluded to the problem of some equating grace with license in 3.8: *And why not do evil that good may come?—as some people slanderously charge us with saying. Their condemnation is just.*

There is liberty in Romans 3–5. From this we should find comfort. Unfortunately, some do take these principles and exploit them. It's nothing new. Toward the end of the first century, Jude warned about those who

crept in unnoticed who long ago were designated for this condemnation, ungodly
people, who pervert the grace of our God into sensuality and deny our only
Master and Lord, Jesus Christ, 1.4.

Today, many Americans claim to have a relationship with Jesus, but most
of them look and act with little difference to the world. Is this a result of
the faith-only, easy-to-believe salvation championed by so many of our
evangelical friends? Large numbers of people miss the connection between
justification and sanctification. It does not help when well-known men
make statements like this:

> The Bible clearly teaches that God's love for His people is of such
> magnitude that even those who walk away from the faith have not the
> slightest chance of slipping from His hand.[25]

> Faith is simply the way we say yes to God's free gift of eternal life.
> Faith and salvation are not one and the same anymore than a gift and
> the hand that receives it are the same. Salvation or justification or
> adoption—whatever you wish to call it—stands independently of faith.
> Consequently, God does not require a constant attitude of faith in order
> to be saved-only an act of faith.[26]

Think of the ramifications of these statements. What conclusion will some
individuals form after hearing or reading such a message?

Now, think of a modern evangelical worship service. After a time of praise
and preaching, the speaker will usually extend an invitation, inviting
people in the audience to "make a decision" for Christ and pray the sinner's
prayer, "asking Him into their heart." One writer reflected on his personal
experience with this and then wondered:

> I'm humbly submitting that this might be the main thing contributing
> to our lethargic, apathetic, and consumer based Christianity that's
> plaguing our nation right now. Doesn't it haunt you that this "prayer" is
> never uttered in the New Testament? Have you ever asked yourself why?
> Doesn't it haunt you that people (in the New Testament) never made a
> "decision" but rather gave up all they had to follow Jesus?

(At my church), I think about 15 people would get saved every service.
At this time they were probably a 3,000+ person church with multiple
campuses in a tiny town. I remember thinking after about a year, that
if 15 people were getting "saved" a service in a town of around 20,000
this city should be upside down for Jesus. But Monday through Saturday
nothing seemed much different.

Nothing makes me tremble more at night than knowing there are
millions of people (most likely in churches) who don't know Jesus at all,
and are being led to hell under the pretense that they are "good to go"
because they prayed a prayer. In fact the main reason they stay distant
from Jesus is that they think they've already "taken care of that." The
truth is, if a boulder dropped on top of you, you'd look different after
the fact. Why is it then that supposedly when the most glorious, holy,
amazing, and beautiful infinite God of the universe "drops" on us we
don't look any different? **You are saved by grace, but real grace changes
you**. [emphasis mine][27]

I bolded the last sentence of that quote, because it goes far in identifying the
missing component. A proper understanding of grace will change a person.
But, the post-modern mindset has infiltrated the pulpits and congregations
of our country. When the message of what it means to **really** conform
to the way of Christ is preached, many receive it as being "judgmental."
Wishing to attract as many as possible, some ministers stand down. While
their listeners go away feeling good about themselves, their listeners have
done little to allow God to conform them to the image of Christ. We
truly live in a time when individuals who claim Jesus as their Savior know
nothing about genuine Christianity. Mainstream religion is doing little to
call individuals to be changed from being *lovers of self, … proud, arrogant,
… ungrateful, unholy, … without self-control,* and are … *lovers of pleasure
rather than lovers of God, having the appearance of godliness, but denying its
power …* 2 Timothy 3.2–5. In fact, it feels as if some are working overtime
to conform Christianity to modern culture.

In response to this easy-to-believe idea, others react by moving equally as far in the opposite direction. (This perspective equates grace with license and forces adherents to live by the rule of law.) In this case, it is thought that rules will make people conform to spirituality. Expectations are forced down the throats of individuals by externalizing the rules. Too often this leads to nothing more than behavior modification with little engagement of the heart. This perspective completely misses God's better way. **External rules do not make people spiritual**. (In Chapter 12, we will take an in-depth look at some of the external rules some have created to enforce on themselves and especially on other Christians they know.)

So what is God's better way?

The Motivation of Grace

The Bible is filled with warnings urging the need for repentance. ...*The unrighteous will not inherit the kingdom of God,* 1 Corinthians 6.9a. This fact should not be ignored. But, it should not be forgotten that God wants His people to move beyond reaching out for Him because of the fear of hell. We need to grow and develop the type of love for Him that cannot be denied. Fear will only take a person so far. Love and appreciation for the goodness of God are far greater motivators. God designed His powerful message of redemption to motivate us to action. Rather than becoming a license to do as we please, grace trains us *to renounce ungodliness and worldly passions, and to live self-controlled, upright, and godly lives in the present age,* Titus 2.12. Grace is an incredible motivator. For example:

God's grace brings salvation from the power of sin. Your salvation is not just about deliverance from a fiery, eternal hell. God longs to deliver you from the love of and desire to sin. He promises rescue from the habit of sin. For those dwelling in misery, chained to the weight of sin, there is no more hopeful message. God offers renewal, making us *a new creation,* 2 Corinthians 5.17. This promise is available to every person, no matter who they are and what they have done. It doesn't matter who you are and what you've been into, you can always come to the cross. God can equip every person to move ahead with holy thoughts, pure speech, and righteous acts that glorify Him.

The principle of love possesses great power over men. Throughout history, governments have erected a myriad of laws in hopes of curbing crime. Even with an understanding of the possibility of the severest consequence, men and women still commit murder. Lawmakers have established harsh penalties for rape, robbery, illegal drug use, and drunk driving. Each year the number of laws passed to curb crime grows. And yet, there has never been a shortage in crime.

> Law commands obedience, but does not promote it. It often creates disobedience, and an over-weighted penalty has been known to provoke an offense. Law fails, but love wins.[28]

How? Consider that:

Love makes sin infamous. Why does no person today name their son Judas? When we think of Judas' sin, we think of the highest treachery. Why? Because He betrayed the Person who is the essence of love and care. **In the light of love, sin is seen to be exceedingly sinful**.

Love has a great constraining power towards the highest form of virtue. Actions to which a person could not be compelled to on the ground of law, have been cheerfully complied with because of love. Goodness wins the heart. Did not Paul write, *For one will scarcely die for a righteous person— though perhaps **for a good person** one would dare even to die*, Romans 5.7 [emphasis mine]. How many are the instances where men and women have willingly sacrificed themselves in order to save someone they loved?

> Duty holds the fort, but love casts its body in the way of the deadly bullet. Who would think of sacrificing his life on the ground of law? Love alone counts not life so dear as the service of the beloved. Love for Christ creates a heroism of which law knows nothing.

Acts of kindness have the power to change the hardest of hearts. This principle is borne out in Scripture:

> To the contrary, "if your enemy is hungry, feed him; if he is thirsty, give him
> something to drink; for by so doing you will heap burning coals on his head."
> Do not be overcome by evil, but overcome evil with good.

— Romans 12.20–21

Why does God expect this from His children? **Grace leads to goodness**. *As bad as men are, the key of their hearts hangs on the nail of love.* God's grace has the power to triumph over the hardest of hearts.

What Does It Mean to Die to Sin?

When we truly see God as He is and understand the power of His salvation, we will want to have nothing more to do with sin. The Sermon on the Mount is a call for a changed heart that yearns for God and His righteousness. *Blessed are the poor in spirit, for theirs is the kingdom of heaven. Blessed are those who mourn, for they shall be comforted. Blessed are the meek, for they shall inherit the earth,* Matthew 5.3-5. What motivated those in the first century to become Christians? Reading through Acts you see men and women who responded when they saw their desperate need for God. They longed to be delivered from sin. They quickly acted in a faith based response—repenting, confessing, and being immersed for *the remission of sin,* Acts 2.38–41; 4.4; 8.31-38; 16.25–33. These individuals understood immersion to be the line of demarcation between the old life that was and what is made new through Christ. Ananias told Saul to *Rise and be baptized, and wash away your sins, calling on His name,* 22.16. The thought of the freedom that comes from being completely finished with one's past can be quite motivating.

Time and time again, the New Testament writers reminded Christians that what was, is no more. As a Christian, you are totally new. Think of yourself for a moment.

- **What you once identified with is no more**. Once you walked *following the course of this world, following the prince of the power of the air,* Ephesians 2.2. But not now. There was a moment when you *died to sin,* Romans 6.2.

- **Where you were is no more**. Your soul has taken up a new residence. Previously dwelling inside *the domain of darkness,* it is in the waters of baptism that God transferred you *into the kingdom of His beloved Son,* Colossians 1.13; 2.11-14.

- **Who you live for has changed.** You no longer live for yourself, but *for Him, who for* (your) *sake died and was raised,* 2 Corinthians 5.15.

Since these things are true, *set your mind on things that are above, not on things that are on earth. **For you have died, and your life is hidden with Christ in God,** Colossians 3.2–3* [emphasis mine]. Death and life are incompatible. You cannot be dead and alive. In Romans 6, Paul's intention is to convey the message that it is completely contradictory for a Christian to be living in sin when he has died to it. At the moment we were baptized, we made a definite break with sin. Sin no longer defines you. Now, God defines you. **Jesus not only died for what you did, but He died to make you who you are.**

When Did We Die to Sin?

When did we *die to sin?* Romans 6.3–6 gives the answer: **upon our baptism into Christ**. It is the undeniable and essential link between our justification and the holy life that results from it.

Baptism is much more than just the end of a five-step checklist. It does not result in God somehow owing us salvation. Rather, it is our loving, faith-filled response to God's extension of grace. Baptism is the link that inseparably ties justification with sanctification. **It is the beginning of a relationship.** Baptism:

- **Brings you into union with Christ.** Your new life has been completely fused into Jesus. He is the Lord over your life and brings you into fellowship with the Father, Ephesians 2.19. You are *one spirit* with Him, 1 Corinthians 6.17. In Galatians, Paul would write, *It is no longer I who live, but Christ who lives in me,* Galatians 2.20b. This fact is inseparably tied to baptism. *For as many of you as were baptized into Christ have put on Christ,* Galatians 3.27. When you were immersed into Christ, you arrayed yourself with Him. You were placed into a new environment: intimate, personal fellowship with the Savior.

- **Allows you to walk in newness of life.** *Newness* refers to "quality" of life. The old prophet Ezekiel looked forward to receiving a *new heart,* and a *new spirit,* Ezekiel 36.26. Paul called it a *new creation,* 2 Corinthians 5.17; a *new creature,* Galatians 6.15; and a *new man,* Ephesians 4.24. Revelation 2.17 says we have received a *new name.* We even sing a *new song,* Psalm 40.3. **Everything is new.** We are a new creation that lives differently from the way we used to. Now, we live like Jesus—moving in holiness, 1 Peter 1.14–16.

With these things being true, **never forget that your new life is the result of the work of God**. Your new birth is a divine accomplishment. It is not by your own power that you have been saved. It is by your faith **in His power to save** that has resulted in your justification. *In him also you were circumcised with a circumcision made without hands, by putting off the body of the flesh, by the circumcision of Christ, having been buried with him in baptism, **in which you were also raised with him through faith in the powerful working of God,** who raised him from the dead,* Colossians 2.11–12 [emphasis mine].

Move Forward with a Knowledge of Who You Are

Many Christians struggle because they fail to realize who they are. Never forget that you are now identified by your association with Jesus. Consider Paul's teaching in Ephesians 4. He begins by describing the Gentiles.

They were *darkened in their understanding* and *alienated from the life of God* because of *ignorance* and *hardness of heart.* They were *callous* and gave *themselves up to sensuality.* They greedily practiced *every kind of impurity,* 4.18-19. Then Paul draws a contrast. *But that is not the way you learned Christ!* 4.20. **You did not learn Christ to continue in sin!** The *putting off* in 4.22 is not so much of a command as it is a statement of fact. You have been recreated *after the likeness of God in true righteousness and holiness,* 4.24. Think of how this connects to Romans 6.6: *our old self was crucified with Him in order that the body of sin might be brought to nothing, so that we would no longer be enslaved to sin.* The expectation is that we must choose to live according to our new identity. *So ... consider yourselves dead to sin and alive to God in Christ Jesus,* Romans 6.11.

Satan is no longer in control of your life. He is no longer the tyrant that calls the shots. You are no longer a slave of sin. You do not have to sin. Choose to follow the direction of Jesus. This is the point of Paul's teaching throughout the rest of Romans 6. When we adopt these principles we can live with the greatest assurance because our heart is connected to God.

- **Decide to refuse to allow sin to dominate your life.** Resist its passions, 6.12. This does not mean that sin will not be a force to be reckoned with. But, remember you have made the decision to no longer place yourself as a slave to it, 6.17.

- **Choose to present your body to God as an instrument for righteousness**, 6.13. This has to do with human will. You can use your body as an instrument to sin or you can use it as an instrument of righteousness, Ephesians 4.24. The Holy Spirit calls on you to yield your will to God. When you do so, this builds assurance. *If you know these things, blessed are you if you do them,* John 13.17.

- **Remember sin no longer has dominion over you.** You are no longer under law, but grace, 6.14. This fact is not encouragement to sin, it is a motivator for holiness, 6.15. *In your hearts honor Christ the Lord as holy,* 1 Peter 3.15a.

- **You have become a slave of righteousness,** 6.16-18. In these verses, two masters are personified. One is sin. The other is obedience. These are the only two options. There is no middle ground. You will either choose to obey God or Satan. Isn't this the teaching of Matthew 6.24? When you became a Christian, you made a commitment to make Jesus Lord of your life. As you practice righteousness it *leads to sanctification,* 6.19. Paul goes on to say the fruit of your new lifestyle leads to *sanctification and its end, eternal life,* 6.22b.

This does not mean that you will never sin again. But the pattern of obedience will become your way of life. **Whatever dominates you is indicative of who your master is.**

Conclusion:

Never forget that you are a living statue of the reality of the gospel.[29] ... *You who were once slaves of sin have become obedient from the heart to the standard of teaching to which you were committed,* 6.17. Notice this doctrine has not been delivered to us. **We have been delivered into it.** *Standard* in the ESV is translated as *form* in the NASU. That word may help us to better understand the meaning of this passage. In the original language, this refers to a "casting mold," "a model," or "a type."[30] Adam Clarke writes:

> Here Christianity is under the notion of a mold, or die, into which they were cast, and from which they took the impression of its excellence. The figure upon this die is the image of God, righteousness, and true holiness, which was stamped on their souls in believing the gospel and receiving the Holy Ghost. The words ... refer to the melting of metal, which, when it is liquefied, is cast into the mold, so that it may receive the impression that is sunk or cut into the mold, and therefore the words that may be literally translated, into which mold of doctrine you have been cast. They were melted down under the preaching of the word, and then were capable of receiving the stamp of its purity.[31]

Before, we were slaves to sin, molded in its ways. But at our baptism, we were rendered into the mold of the gospel and received the impression of it. Think of it in this way. The grace of God melted your heart. And when you reached out to God in this soft and pliable condition, God placed you into His mold. Now, God expects you to live according to the pattern of truth that is the gospel. God has stamped you with the image of Christ, Romans 8.29.

"People live the way they learn to live." Think of this in practical terms. You came out of a certain family and you bear the image of that family. Now, spiritually, you are in God's family. He will teach you how to live. That's the goal of discipleship. *But everyone when he is fully trained will be like His teacher,* Luke 6.40b. Paul said, *do not be **conformed** to this world,* Romans 12.2a [emphasis mine]. Instead, you have been poured into a new mold in the form of sound teaching, 12.2b. Now, you live inside a new reality. "Only God could melt down the old person and pour the ingredients back into a new mold and shape that new person."[32]

Pause for a moment and give God thanks. Now, go forward living inside the new reality He has created for you.

For Thought and Reflection:

1. Describe the two extremes presented in the introduction. What are the main problems associated with each viewpoint?

2. What does grace teach us to do?

3. In what way is grace a motivator? How is this viewpoint superior to the perspective that operates primarily from the basis of law-keeping?

4. As a Christian, you are totally new, 2 Corinthians 5.17. What are three important things you must remember as you live for Christ?

5. When did you die to sin? What verses in Romans 6 demonstrate this fact?

6. What did your baptism do?

7. By whose power were you saved?

8. Why is it so important for you to move forward with an understanding of your new identity?

9. What is the result of practicing righteousness? See 6.19, 22.

10. What is the goal of discipleship?

The Struggle with Flesh and Spirit

Introduction:

Has Satan had his way with you lately? Are you struggling with some weakness of the flesh? Even though you've asked God for forgiveness, do you still feel deflated?

As Christians go through the process of being conformed to the image of Christ, they experience a lifelong struggle with the flesh. We are all aware of spiritual warfare inside our lives. Romans 7 contains writing by a great spiritual leader who endured this struggle.

> *For I do not understand my own actions. For I do not do what I want, but I do the very thing I hate. For I do not do the good I want, but the evil I do not want is what I keep on doing. Now if I do what I do not want, it is no longer I who do it, but sin that dwells within me. So I find it to be a law that when I want to do right, evil lies close at hand. For I delight in the law of God, in my inner being, but I see in my members another law waging war against the law of my mind and making me captive to the law of sin that dwells in my members. Wretched man that I am! Who will deliver me from this body of death?*
>
> — Romans 7.15, 19–24

There is much controversy associated with this passage. Is this Paul reflecting on his life before Christ? Some say there is entirely too much desire for sin here for this to be the testimony of a Christian. Verses 14, 17-18, and 24 leads a person to conclude that this is a man totally under the power of sin, separated from Christ. After all, there are other passages where Paul wrote that *we were in the flesh, 7.5,* and *we have been released from the Law, having died to that which we were bound, so that we serve in newness of the Spirit, 7.6.* It was Paul who just wrote *sin shall not be master over you, 6.14.* So, if all these things are true, how can 7.15, 19-24 describe a Christian?

In Romans 7, Paul's writing seems to be very far from where we understand salvation. Refer to Romans 6 where he wrote:

- **6.2** — we have died to sin.

- **6.6** — the old self was crucified, the body of sin has been done away with, we are no longer slaves of sin.

- **6.7** — we have died and are freed from sin.

- **6.11** — dead to sin.

- **6.12** — no need to let sin reign in our mortal bodies.

- **6.13** — do not go on presenting the members of your body as instruments of unrighteousness.

- **6.17-18** — we were slaves of sin, but have become obedient from the heart … having been free from sin and have become slaves of righteousness.

- **6.22** — we have been freed from sin and enslaved to God.

All of these passages say that sin has lost its power and so it would seem that what is written in chapter 7 could never describe a faithful Christian.

But yet, there is a very clear indication in Romans 6 that there is still a battle that rages. Look again at 6.12: *Let not sin therefore reign in your mortal body, to make you obey its passions. Do not present your members to sin as instruments for unrighteousness, but present yourselves to God as those who have been brought from death to life, and your members to God as instruments for righteousness.* This implies that each Christian has the responsibility to act against sin as it is confronted in daily life.

Those who understand Romans 7 as a description of Paul's life as he struggled as a Christian see things from a different perspective. Consider 7.22: *For I delight in the law of God, in my inner being.* This statement is significant. It reflects a heart that wants to obey God. Deep down, Paul had been changed, but he still battled the flesh. 7.25 also gives us a glimpse of a changed heart. *I myself serve the law of God with my mind.* Other passages also seem to indicate the personal, day to day battle that Christians face:

- **7.15** — Paul liked to do certain things, but he did not do them. He hated to do other things and did them anyway.

- **7.16** — He agreed with the law and knew it was good.

- **7.19** — The good that he wished to do he did not do and did the evil he did not want to do. (Inside Paul was a powerful desire for obedience, to honor, obey, and serve God.)

- **7.21** — He wished to do good.

While cases can be made on both sides of this issue, the bottom line is that Paul faced a battle between what he delighted in and what he actually did.

This has to be the battle of a transformed soul. The more sensitive he became to the demands of God's holiness and righteousness, the more he saw the contradiction existing inside himself. And as he progressed through the process of sanctification, the more painful it was for him to see what he **really is** in spite of what he wants. *Wretched man that I am!* 7.24. This is an honest expression of pain over the struggle to fulfill his deepest longings. This is clearly the writing of a Christian. It describes an inevitable tension in life that we must not ignore.

Every believer feels the agony of this struggle. While we love righteousness, 7.19, 21, and delight in God's law, 7.22, we also deeply regret our sins. We long for a time when God will deliver us, 7.25. Each one of us lives with two extremes, which are held in tension. We are human and subject to the conditions of mortal life. But, yet, we are God's spiritual people who have passed from darkness into life. We are new creations. We are in Christ. And yet the flesh remains. Even though he was a very mature Christian, Paul was very conscious of the alluring power of sin which still tried to dictate things opposite of his own desires. For the rest of his life he would struggle with this and never fully overcome it. *For the desires of the flesh are against the Spirit, and the desires of the Spirit are against the flesh, for these are opposed to each other, to keep you from doing the things you want to do,* Galatians 5.17.

This is the Christian life. Paul fought it just like every other Christian does.

As You Struggle, Remember Who You Are

It is very common for Christians who fight fierce battles with the flesh to dwell in disappointment. When we do, it is important to remember our righteousness.

- **You have been made new**, 2 Corinthians 5.17. Now, you walk in newness of life, Romans 6.4.

- **You have eternal life**, Titus 3.7.

- **You have become fit for the presence of God**, Ephesians 2.19.

- **You have *purified* your *soul by* your *obedience to the truth*,** 1 Peter 1.22. Remember that you have obeyed the gospel. You have believed, repented, and been baptized. In 1.22, *purified* is in present perfect tense, indicating past action with continuing results.

- **You have been washed, purified, and given new life**. When you were baptized, you put on the new man, Ephesians 4.24.

- **You have been recreated for righteousness and holiness**. This birth is not by *perishable seed*, but *imperishable,* 1 Peter 1.22-23.

- **You are now a *partaker of the divine nature*,** 2 Peter 1.4. God has given you a new identity.

We must never steal God's glory by discounting what He has made us. Rather than living in constant disappointment with ourselves, we must choose to live the way Paul does in Romans 7. Upon examining ourselves, we will find we do things we do not want to do. We will do things that are absolutely inconsistent with who we are. As we do, **we need to see that sin as an intrusion into who we really are in Christ**. We must hate the sin we see, confess it to God, and treat it, at best, as an unwelcome guest or at worst, as an invasion by a fierce and threatening enemy.

But that is no longer who you are. **Sin no longer defines who you are.**
You have been redeemed as Christ's own possession. You *want to do what
is good*. You *do not want to do what is evil*. You want to serve the law of God.
This is who you are in Christ. Paul looked forward to the day he would be
delivered from his body of sin and death, Romans 7.24. Death will involve
separation from the physical body. You will be liberated from the flesh and
set free to be everything you were created to be when you were made new
in Christ.

I love the hit song by Matthew West, released in early 2013, that is played
on Christian contemporary radio stations. The lyrics go far in reminding us
of who we are:

> *Hello, my name is regret. I'm pretty sure we have met. Every single day of
> your life, I'm the whisper inside, That won't let you forget.*

> *Hello, my name is defeat. I know you recognize me. Just when you think you
> can win, I'll drag you right back down again, 'Til you've lost all belief.*

> *These are the voices, these are the lies. And I have believed them,
> for the very last time.*

> *Hello, my name is child of the one true King. I've been saved, I've been changed,
> and I have been set free. "Amazing Grace" is the song I sing.*

> *Hello, my name is child of the one true King. I am no longer defined By all the
> wreckage behind. The one who makes all things new has proven it's true.*

> *Just take a look at my life. What love the Father has lavished upon us That we
> should be called His children. I am a child of the one true King.*[33]

How to Have Victory against Your Flesh

Remembering who we are should drive us to resist the flesh. Indeed we
must *crucify the flesh with its passions*, Galatians 5.24. We must value the
spiritual over the fleshly. What can you do to have victory over your flesh?

Fill your life with God's word. Hebrews 4.12 describes God's word as alive. It is God's energetic power to transform. It is a discerner *of the thoughts and intentions of the heart.* Scripture gives us God's viewpoint about our lives. He has designed His word to help us purify our lives, so we can live in harmony with Him. God wants us to sacrifice the desires of the flesh thereby cleaning up our lives. His intention is not just to make us *comfortable.* Scripture is the perfect agent to get into the hard to reach places and clean out destructive thoughts that decay or weaken our strength to become all that God wants for us.

Learn self-control. Understand that every fleshly temptation has a friend. Every choice has a consequence. Usually, self-control fades as we allow our emotions to take control. This is Satan's desire. He wants you to deny God and make your choices based on emotion. *"This feels right"* has damaged more spiritual relationships and caused more pain than perhaps any other excuse. In the moment, temptation appears to fill a need, but in the end it leads to guilt and shame. So, practice self-control like Paul did, 1 Corinthians 9.27. He *disciplined* his *body and* kept *it under control.* He calls on every Christian to resist: … *For just as you once presented your members as slaves to impurity and to lawlessness leading to more lawlessness, so now present your members as slaves to righteousness leading to sanctification,* Romans 6.19.

Make conscious choices to avoid situations that arouse your flesh. Psalm 101 contains very good advice from David:

- 101.3 — *I will not set before my eyes anything that is worthless. I hate the work of those who fall away; it shall not cling to me.* [emphasis mine]

- 101.4 — *A perverse heart shall be far from me; I will know nothing of evil.* [emphasis mine]

- 101.6 — *I will look with favor on the faithful in the land,* that they may dwell with me; he who walks in the way that is blameless shall minister to me. [emphasis mine]

- 101.7 — **No one who practices deceit shall dwell in my house**; *no one who utters lies shall continue before my eyes.* [emphasis mine]

Conclusion:

So what will you choose? What do you value more? Your flesh? Or your spirit? This is the great conflict of life. Will we trust enough in God's power to transform us? Will we trust that one day we will be separated from this body of death and be completely *blameless and holy* in His sight? Will this trust be evidenced through the actions of an obedient life that lives to put on holiness and righteousness? See 1 Peter 1.14-25.

Jesus died to redeem you from sin and make you new. He has given you a new identity. Now that He has, *crucify the flesh with its passions,* Galatians 5.24.

For Thought and Reflection:

1. What is the Christian's responsibility toward sin?

2. Inwardly, what did Paul desire to do?

3. How did Paul feel about the sins he committed?

4. In this life, can we ever fully overcome the struggle with the flesh? Why? Why not?

5. What is important about the word *purified* in 1 Peter 1.22?

6. What have you been recreated for? See Ephesians 1.4.

7. How must we view sin in our life?

8. When will we be delivered from fleshly desires?

9. How can you develop a deeper sense of value toward spiritual things?

10. What are some worthless things we set before our eyes?

11. How can we learn from David's resolve to resist the flesh?

12. What do you honestly value more? The flesh? Or the spirit.

There Is No Condemnation for Those Who Are in Christ

Introduction:

There is therefore now no condemnation for those who are in Christ Jesus.
For the law of the Spirit of life has set you free in Christ Jesus from
the law of sin and death.

— Romans 8.1–2

C hristians have been adopted into the family of God. *Adoption* is a powerful word. It describes a concept that is filled with love, mercy, and grace. When an adoption happens, a person is taken into a family that is not related to them and given all the rights and privileges as a member of that family. If you've experienced adoption in relation to your physical family, you know it is just something truly incredible. I know this from personal experience. On May 5, 1974 my biological father was killed in a hunting accident directly in front of my mother. The emotional trauma of that day still has an effect on her. Only a little over 9 weeks old, I never knew my father. My mother, still a newlywed, moved back in with her parents. It was a very dark time for my family. Two years later, mom met Sam Allen, who she would later marry. Sam (dad) adopted me. Ever since, I've been welcomed as if I were a flesh and blood member of the Allen family. It's been such a blessing. In 2013, mom and dad gave me the adoption document that was signed by a judge in 1980. I love the language of the last paragraph of the judge's writing:

> IT IS THEREFORE BY THE COURT CONSIDERED AND
> ORDERED, that Joseph Matthew Harvey Allen be and he is hereby
> permanently adopted to the Petitioners, Sam Allen and Donna Allen,
> his natural mother, for all intents and purposes as though he had been
> the natural child of both; that the Bureau of Vital Statistics of the State
> Health Department of Arkansas should be and hereby is authorized and

directed to substitute the child's birth certificate showing the Petitioners as his parents. IT IS SO ORDERED.

I have been very blessed by the graciousness of my father, Sam Allen, who brought me into his family. I will be forever thankful for God's direction in bringing him into my life.

There are many stories of adoption in the Bible. There are at least three instances occurring in the Old Testament. Moses (Exodus 2) and Esther (Esther 2) are two examples. But perhaps the most compelling story of adoption is seen in 2 Samuel 9 with David's adoption of Saul's grandson: Mephibosheth. Saul had been the continual enemy of David, doing everything he could to kill him. Saul's jealousy, hatred, and pride are almost unrivaled. The character of Saul stands in great contrast to his son Jonathan—who was David's closest friend and confidant. At the age of five, Mephibosheth was paralyzed when he was dropped by his caretaker, 2 Samuel 4.4. After David came to power, what was left of the family of Saul fell out of the spotlight.

David took the initiative and extended kindness to the sons of Jonathan. They searched the kingdom and found Mephibosheth, who dwelled in Lo-debar or "the barren land." There was nothing worse in society than to be crippled. Mephibosheth offered nothing to society. Even the meaning of his name ("A Shameful Thing") indicated his low place in the world. He was from the family of an enemy. When David moved to adopt Mephibosheth, it was truly an act of grace, 2 Samuel 9.6–7. Because of David's kindness and love, in which Mephibosheth did nothing to earn, he was able to come and go inside the palace *as one of the king's sons,* 9.11b. In a culture that ostracized the crippled and lame, Mephibosheth ate at the king's table! It's an incredible story of grace!

Other than God's demonstration of grace and mercy to sinners, there is perhaps no better story in the Bible related to adoption than this. David's adoption of Mephibosheth is how God adopts us today. By sending His son, God took the initiative and showed mercy to those who are unworthy,

Romans 5.6. God moves to save us by His incredible love and kindness, Ephesians 2.6–7. God redeemed us when we were far outside the realm of perfection and gave us an inheritance, 1 Peter 1.3–4. This adoption is for all who will separate themselves unto the Lord and *cleanse themselves,* 2 Corinthians 6.17 – 7.1.

In Romans 8, Paul moved to establish how Christians have assurance in their salvation. We stand in and live by grace. We've been adopted into the family of God. Notice the terminology used in Romans 8.14–16: *For all who are led by the Spirit of God are **sons of God***. *For you did not receive the spirit of slavery to fall back into fear, but you have received the Spirit of **adoption as sons**, by whom we cry, "Abba! Father!" The Spirit himself bears witness with our spirit that we are **children of God*** [emphasis mine]. These terms are significant. And, they should go a long way in quelling any fears we have that are related to our status as sons and daughters of God.

Think about it in terms of ancient kings "adopting" a successor or when passing the rule to his own son, declaring: "This is my own son." This gives us a greater depth of understanding in what means to be sons and daughters of God!

The idea of adoption and sonship extends to the point of joint rule with Christ. This is seen in Paul's thoughts in Ephesians 1.15 – 2.10. The *Father of glory* raised Jesus and seated him at his right hand. We have been made alive (2.5), raised up by the power that raised Jesus and seated with Christ, 2.6. This is *the immeasurable greatness of his power toward us who believe, according to the working of his great might that he worked in Christ when he raised him from the dead* … 1.19–20. Christ is seated at the right hand of God. We are seated with Christ. We are enthroned with him. We are restored to the rule for which we were created! See Genesis 1.26, 28.

Romans 8: Security in Christ

There is a powerful truth communicated in Romans 8.1. It is carried throughout the chapter. Those who walk in the light no longer have to pay the penalty for sin; it has been paid by the blood of Jesus Christ. No one besides ourselves can take our status away.

> Who is to condemn? Christ Jesus is the one who died—more than that, who was raised—who is at the right hand of God, who indeed is interceding for us. Who shall separate us from the love of Christ? Shall tribulation, or distress, or persecution, or famine, or nakedness, or danger, or sword? No, in all these things we are more than conquerors through him who loved us.
>
> — Romans 8.34–35, 37

Can you see Paul's confidence? Did you observe his assurance? Salvation is only possible by the work of Jesus. Our new status in Christ is continually confirmed by the Holy Spirit. Inside Chapter 8, there are seven ways the Spirit works to assure us of our position in God's kingdom:

- **8.2-3** — The Spirit sets us free from sin and death.

- **8.4** — The Spirit enables us to fulfill the law.

- **8.5-11** — The Spirit assists us in our sanctification.

- **8.12-13** — The Spirit equips and empowers us for victory.

- **8.14-16** — The Spirit confirms our adoption.

- **8.17-25** — The Spirit guarantees our victory.

- **8.26-27** — The Spirit intercedes for us.

Those who have been adopted into Christ have had their former debt of sin washed away. Christians belong to God. He has established our right to be in His presence. We are possessors of His kingdom. These facts are confirmed in our hearts. *The Spirit himself bears witness with our spirit that we are children of God*, Romans 8.16.

While we can know objectively that we are sons and daughters of God, there is also subjective assurance. How does God confirm our adoption?

We Are Led by the Spirit

For all who are led by the Spirit of God are sons of God, Romans 8.14. As
you examine your life, can you see God's Spirit working? We are not
speaking of some mysterious presence of God. We are looking for tangible
evidence of the work of God. One example is found through examining our
conduct. Are you molding your conduct into the ways of Christ? Are you
experiencing victory over sin and temptation? *For if you live according to
the flesh you will die, but if by the Spirit you put to death the deeds of the body,
you will live,* Romans 8.13. The power of any victory you experience **comes
from God** and this reality proves you are being led by His Spirit.

Are you cooperating with the Spirit? Have you submitted to the leadership
of God? He will lead and change your will—**if you let Him.** There are a
number of passages that speak of the leading of God:

- **Proverbs 3.5-6** — *He will make straight your paths...*

- **Psalm 25.4, 9; 143.10** — God not only leads the lives of His
  children—He teaches them to obey His leading.

- **Jeremiah 10.23** — it is not within us to direct our own steps. We trust
  Him, not ourselves.

The Spirit leads the Christian **through the word of God**. Ask:

Am I allowing my mind and heart to be open to what it says?

Will I make time to read and meditate on it?

Will I allow it to fill my heart?

Does God's word totally dominate your thinking? *And so, from the day we
heard, we have not ceased to pray for you, asking that you may be filled with the
knowledge of his will in all spiritual wisdom and understanding,* Colossians 1.9.
Filled in 1.9 means to "cram" our heart with knowledge. Learn to discern
His principles (spiritual wisdom) and move with action (understanding).
There are tangible effects of allowing the Spirit to fill your heart:

- **Colossians 1.10a** — You *walk in a manner worthy of the Lord*, striving to be *fully pleasing to him.*

- **Colossians 1.10b** — You *(bear) fruit in every good work.*

- **Colossians 1.10c** — You will *(increase) in the knowledge of God.* The idea is to move with an eye on spiritual maturity.

- **Colossians 1.11a** — You will be *strengthened with all power, according to his glorious might.* God does not just act with reference to your initial salvation. He wants to interact with you continually, equipping you for your entire journey to heaven.

- **Colossians 1.11b** — You will gain *endurance and patience with joy.*

This is why Christians have been instructed to *let the word of Christ dwell in you richly,* Colossians 3.16. The Spirit of God will illuminate the word. It will become living to us as we seek to apply it to our lives. The filling of our minds with the knowledge of His will is not just done for the sake of gaining knowledge. We do it in order to conform our lives to the will of God. Do you need assurance of your salvation? Ask:

- *Do I understand the word of God?* Do you pray regularly for better understanding and illumination in difficult passages? God's principles and expectations must be allowed to shape and mold your heart! *Is God opening the truths of His word to your heart?*

- *Do I see the reality (authority) of His word?*

- *Does it bring me joy? Is my heart touched with conviction?*

We must actively respond to the leading of God through the word. *Lead me in the path of your commandments, for I delight in it. Keep steady my steps according to your promise, and let no iniquity get dominion over me,* Psalm 119.35, 133.

The leading by God through the application of His word is sanctification. Sanctification is the *process of spiritual separation unto God in acts of obedience.*[34] This process is **continual.** Being **led by the Spirit refers to a way of life.** It is not a one-time experience. We allow the process to continue every day. In other words, we must respond to the work of the Spirit and not resist it. See 1 Thessalonians 5.19 and Ephesians 4.30. If we choose to sin and move away from God, there will be no assurance of our salvation. We will have no confidence.

But this is not the normal course for a child of God who has his or her heart set on God. For them, the Spirit wants to affirm their place inside the family of God. As we follow His leading, we will enjoy all the affirmation we need.

We Are Freed by the Spirit

For you did not receive the spirit of slavery to fall back into fear, but you have received the Spirit of adoption as sons, by whom we cry, "Abba! Father!" Romans 8.15. God has liberated Christians from the bondage of fear! Too many Christians live in bondage, fearing punishment, worrying they have not done enough for God. Some worry about coming up short in the end. **God did not come into your life to bring you that.** Romans 8 has been placed in Scripture for a purpose. Christians belong to God! *There is no fear in love, but perfect love casts out fear. For fear has to do with punishment, and whoever fears has not been perfected in love,* 1 John 4.18. Who has loved us with a perfect love? God. Jesus is the ultimate expression of that love. Because of His work, we have nothing to fear!

God has placed the Spirit in your life to bring confirmation of your status in His kingdom. He has set your heart free from the fear of punishment and judgment. He has liberated you! You have access to a tender, intimate, and loving relationship with the eternal Father. Paul used the expression of *Abba Father* to describe this very personal relationship. God lives to interact with you!

The Spirit Bears Witness

The Spirit himself bears witness with our spirit that we are children of God, Romans 8.16. It does not matter what anyone else says. Even if Satan accuses you with all his might and tells all manner of lies—you belong to God! *Who shall bring any charge against God's elect? It is God who justifies. Who is to condemn? Christ Jesus is the one who died—more than that, who was raised—who is at the right hand of God, who indeed is interceding for us. Who shall separate us from the love of Christ?* Romans 8.33-35a. The Spirit wants you to have an intimacy with God. How does the Spirit bear witness of your salvation?

One way is through obedience. 2 Peter 1.4 clearly says Christians have been saved. Because they have been saved, the virtues listed in 1.5-7 come as they walk in the light, follow His leading, and live in the freedom He provides. *For if these qualities are yours and are increasing, they keep you from being ineffective or unfruitful in the knowledge of our Lord Jesus Christ,* 1.8.

But do not stop at 1.8. Those who choose not to walk in the light will find no assurance. *For whoever lacks these qualities is so nearsighted that he is blind, having forgotten that he was cleansed from his former sins,* 1.9. Your assurance comes by fruit produced in a life that walks in the light. If you refuse to walk along God's path, you will become spiritually blind and forget the cleansing you received when you obeyed the gospel.

Conclusion:

God, through His Spirit, continually works to give you assurance in your salvation. Those who walk in the light have no condemnation, Romans 8.1. You can enjoy this as long as you respond to the work of the Spirit through the word, allow God to lead you, and have the kind of attitude that depends on God.

If you choose not to walk in obedience, you will not have assurance. How do you know you are a Christian? Actively abide in His precepts.

Little children, let us not love in word or talk but in deed and in truth. By
this we shall know that we are of the truth and reassure our heart before
him; for whenever our heart condemns us, God is greater than our heart,
and he knows everything. Beloved, if our heart does not condemn us, we
have confidence before God; and whatever we ask we receive from him,
because we keep his commandments and do what pleases him. And this
is his commandment, that we believe in the name of his Son Jesus Christ
and love one another, just as he has commanded us. Whoever keeps his
commandments abides in God, and God in him. And by this we know that he
abides in us, by the Spirit whom he has given us.

— 1 John 3.18–24

Note the last part of 3.24. Who supplies confidence? It is the Spirit, who does this work all the time.

It is hard to imagine the degree of change that Mephibosheth experienced. But we do know it was incredible. Imagine! A crippled man *sitting at the king's table,* eating as *one of the king's sons.* **That's grace!** May we all realize that we are the crippled sinners who now dwell in the house of the Lord! Praise God for His incredible grace!

For Thought and Reflection:

1. What is so beautiful about adoption? What are some examples of adoption in the Bible?

2. Describe the work of the Spirit in Romans 8 to give Christians assurance of their salvation.

3. What does it mean to be *led by the Spirit?*

4. What is the impact of being filled with the knowledge of God?

5. What is key to God's Spirit leading us?

6. Of what has God set us free? See Romans 8.15.

7. How does the Spirit *bear witness* of our salvation? See Romans 8.16.

8. What is the result of our refusal to walk down God's path? See 2 Peter 1.9.

9. How can you know you are a Christian?

10. Today's lesson has helped my assurance by:

The Power of Hope

Introduction:

Hope is the confident expectation of good. The Holy Spirit fills us with knowledge, which brings joy and assurance of eternal salvation, Colossians 1.10-11. We earnestly hope to be raised from death into eternal life. Hope does not have reference to that which we see and have; it looks forward to what we expect to receive.

God is the source of our hope. His mercy is abundant. There has literally been a tremendous outpouring of kindness by God.

> *He does not deal with us according to our sins, nor repay us according to our iniquities. … As far as the east is from the west, so far does he remove our transgressions from us. As a father shows compassion to his children, so the LORD shows compassion to those who fear him. For he knows our frame; he remembers that we are dust.*
>
> — Psalm 103.10, 12–14

In his first epistle, Peter explained how God has taken sinners, who are in a miserable condition, and brought them to Jesus to be delivered from sin. *Blessed be the God and Father of our Lord Jesus Christ! According to his great mercy, he has caused us to be born again to a living hope through the resurrection of Jesus Christ from the dead,* 1 Peter 1.3. Next, Peter described the object of our hope. We look forward to *an inheritance that is imperishable, undefiled, and unfading, kept in heaven for you,* 1 Peter 1.4. Our reward will be free of anything that would render it undesirable. It will be completely free of contamination and decay. This stands in direct contrast to all we see, handle, taste, smell, and hear in this world. Everything is subject to decay and disease. Everything has an end. Our bodies grow frail and eventually die. "Nothing is abiding. The physical form of man with the passing years begins its decay and finally in death will perish."[35] But, our reward will never fade away. Constant in quality, it will never be diminished or dimmed. Time will have no effect in heaven. At the end of 1.4, Peter makes it personal. This reward has been reserved *for you*. **Every faithful Christian will receive this reward.**

1 Peter 1.5 is especially comforting, because **once we receive this hope; it is protected, guarded, and secure.** God will not abandon us to our own devices. He walks with us each step of the way, guarding us through His all-powerful protection. We are those *who by God's power are being guarded through faith for a salvation ready to be revealed in the last time*, 1 Peter 1.5. Not only does the Father play a role in our hope, Jesus does as well, 1 Peter 1.6-9. It is in Jesus that we place our trust. We make a commitment to Him and expect to receive the outcome of our faith, the salvation of our soul, 1 Peter 1.9. Jesus has secured our hope through the power of His resurrection.

In 1 Peter 1.10-12, Peter explains how the Holy Spirit plays a role in our hope. Old Testament prophets predicted that Jesus would suffer and die on the cross for the sins of the world. These prophets of old were moved to speak directly by the Holy Spirit. But, they were not the only ones who served as the mouthpieces of God's good news. In New Testament times, John the Baptist was directed to foretell certain details of Jesus' life. Later, many preached the gospel. These individuals brought forth the good news of salvation through Jesus. This was the work of the Holy Spirit. *And we also thank God constantly for this, that when you received the word of God, which you heard from us, you accepted it not as the word of men but as what it really is, the word of God, which is at work in you believers*, 1 Thessalonians 2.13. We have the writing of these men, revealed by the Spirit, in our Bibles today. Reading God's word can certainly give us hope.

How Important is Hope?

Besides our gratefulness and appreciation for God's grace, our hope is an essential source of motivation for us.

It serves as the anchor of the soul, Hebrews 6.19. It keeps us from being washed away with the onrushing and turbulent waters of life. The hope of heaven most certainly motivated Paul. Each day of his life saw new opportunities to glorify God through persecution and suffering. It was the hope of what awaited him in the life to come that fueled his endurance. *I can do all things through him who strengthens me,* Philippians 4.13.

In the original language, the wording is "I can *endure* all things." The strength supplied by Jesus and the desire for a permanent home in heaven empowered Paul to press through the gravest of persecution. Paul's hope enabled him to sing praises while in jail, Acts 16.25. He and Silas knew their imprisonment was only temporary. Even if they lost their life the next day, they knew a home in heaven awaited.

> *We have this treasure in jars of clay, to show that the surpassing power belongs to God and not to us. We are afflicted in every way, but not crushed; perplexed, but not driven to despair; persecuted, but not forsaken; struck down, but not destroyed; always carrying in the body the death of Jesus, so that the life of Jesus may also be manifested in our bodies.*
> — 2 Corinthians 4.7–10

It gives us something to live for. It becomes our purpose in life; our mission; our plan of action. The severest reality of misery is when our hope is only in this life, 1 Corinthians 15.19. Hope brings us joy and brings life to death. And, it brightens and lifts our feelings. Life without hope is at best, bleak. Those who only have hope in this world are truly most miserable.

Consider Romans 8.18: *For I consider that the sufferings of this present time are not worth comparing with the glory that is to be revealed to us.* Think about it. We possess a salvation in which the greatest part has yet to be revealed. While we can move in thankfulness for our present blessings in Christ, nothing can be compared with the blessings we will experience in the life to come. Later Paul said that we *eagerly await our adoption as sons, the redemption of our bodies.* While our inner person is being renewed day by day, we still have our fleshly body to contend with. As we move through life, we grow to eagerly await the transformation of our body. One day we will be made like Him and see Him just as He is, 1 John 3.2. **We live in this hope.** It was Paul who said, *For in this hope we were saved. Now hope that is seen is not hope. For who hopes for what he sees?* Romans 8.24. Hope is a major component in our salvation.

Our Hope Is in God, Not Self

Our hope is not in men. We do not place it in self. We lay our hope in the unchanging God who always speaks truth. Notice how God is referenced in Psalm 43.5. He is our help. He is our God. He has made real promises of care, concern, protection, guidance, direction, and sustenance. **We can always trust Him for a better tomorrow**. He has promised to meet all of our earthly needs and gives us the promise of eternal life, Psalm 78.7; Matthew 6.25-34.

Another important aspect about our hope is to understand that it is an act of grace. **We do not earn our hope.** *Now may our Lord Jesus Christ himself, and **God our Father,** who loved us and **gave us eternal comfort and good hope through grace,*** 2 Thessalonians 2.16 [emphasis mine]. God is the one who gives us hope, for it is by grace. Praise Him for that!

It is God who secures our hope. In the introduction, we looked at 1 Peter 1.3. Please read that passage again. Notice that our *living hope* is secured by the resurrection of Christ. **If Jesus did not rise, we will not either.** But notice, Jesus said, *Because I live, you also will live,* John 14.19b. Spiritually, we were made alive when we responded to God's call for salvation. We died with Him in the waters of baptism, Romans 6.1–6. When we did so, we rose with Him in newness of life, 2 Corinthians 5.17.

This is all possible, because the God we serve is the God of hope. He is the source of it. *May **the God of hope** fill you with all joy and peace in believing, so that by the power of the Holy Spirit you may abound in hope,* Romans 15.13 [emphasis mine]. Notice that our hope is been graciously given to us, secured by the resurrection of Christ, and here hope is **confirmed by the Holy Spirit**. It is the Spirit working in us through the word that stirs up within us an attitude filled with hope.

The Bible says all three members of the godhead are involved in our hope. The Father **gives** hope. The Son **secured** hope. And, the Spirit **confirms** it. The hope for new life is real because Jesus conquered death for Himself and for all who believe in Him.

Hope Produces Peace

God is our Rock. He is unchangeable. He is a covenant keeping God. He is completely sovereign. This should fill our hearts with peace for several reasons.

Hope defends us from Satan. In 1 Thessalonians 5.8, hope is described as a helmet. This is the same thought that is conveyed in Ephesians 6.10–13 where Paul describes a great spiritual battle that is going on along many different levels. One of the key weapons in Satan's arsenal is to attack us with doubt. He often seeks to smash us in the head—but we have our helmet on. You see, the helmet of hope defends us against the endless attacks of Satan. Every one of us will face this type of attack at one time or another. *Where do we go to be anchored?* **Back to the hope of our salvation.** It provides us with comfort in the knowledge that no matter what happens, there is something better coming.

But, not only is hope a source of comfort, it is a line of defense. The Psalmist said, *I hope in your word,* Psalm 119.114. That is where we must go. The Scripture has been described as a sword, Ephesians 6.17. The writer of Hebrews also describes its power in Hebrews 4.12. Again and again, we need to read and reread what God has prepared for those who love Him.

Hope is confirmed in trials. Are you going through a trial? Are you being continually pounded by doubt? Always remember that *God has not destined us for wrath, but to obtain salvation through our Lord Jesus Christ,*

1 Thessalonians 5.9. It is by this knowledge that we can encourage one another. *Therefore encourage one another and build one another up, just as you are doing,* 5.11.

I think Paul expounds on this in Romans 8. Shortly after the writing of this epistle, the Roman Christians would endure intense persecution. What is written in 8.31-39 would serve as a tremendous source of encouragement for Christians of all time. During trials of any sort, remember that:

- **If God is for us, who can be against us?** 8.31.

- **God has declared us righteous,** 8.32-33.

- **Jesus is interceding for us,** 8.34-35. *Nothing can separate us from the love of Christ.*

- **We will be more than conquerors,** 8.37.

Trials have a way of strengthening our hope. When we have the right attitude, they can make our hope brighter, because through them we can see the steady and secure hand of God.

Hope produces pure joy. When you have built the foundation of your life on God, you will have the purest joy. *Blessed is the man who trusts in the LORD, whose trust is the LORD. He is like a tree planted by water, that sends out its roots by the stream, and does not fear when heat comes, for its leaves remain green, and is not anxious in the year of drought, for it does not cease to bear fruit,* Jeremiah 17.7-8. It was the Psalmist who said, *Blessed is he whose hope is in the Lord his God,* Psalm 146.5. Nothing hinders God's purposes.

Hope removes fear of death. A Christian learns to view death as a release, not an end. It is the fulfillment of hope! Death brings our entrance into the world God has called us to. It frees us up to be what we were redeemed to be. *When the perishable puts on the imperishable, and the mortal puts on immortality, then shall come to pass the saying that is written: 'Death is swallowed up in victory.' 'O death, where is your victory? O death, where is your sting?'* 1 Corinthians 15.54-55. This hope is absolutely fixed, Titus 1.2. **God cannot lie**.

Since all of these things are true, *Do not be anxious about anything, but in everything by prayer and supplication with thanksgiving let your requests be made known to God. And the peace of God, which surpasses all understanding, will guard your hearts and your minds in Christ Jesus*, Philippians 4.6-7. Peace that surpasses all understanding comes by turning to God. He is our shield and impenetrable defense.

While passing through the sea of life, our boat may be rocked by trial, temptation, and sin. But, no matter what happens, we know God loves us and will protect us. He never leaves our side! Even if we lose everything in this life, we still have our hope! No one in this life can take that away. *For I am sure that neither death nor life, nor angels nor rulers, nor things present nor things to come, nor powers, nor height nor depth, nor anything else in all creation, will be able to separate us from the love of God in Christ Jesus our Lord,* Romans 8.38-39. Even during the Old Testament time, those who had fully given themselves to God lived with a confident hope.

> *The LORD is my light and my salvation; whom shall I fear? The LORD is the stronghold of my life; of whom shall I be afraid? When evildoers assail me to eat up my flesh, my adversaries and foes, it is they who stumble and fall. Though an army encamp against me, my heart shall not fear; though war arise against me, yet I will be confident. One thing have I asked of the LORD, that will I seek after: that I may dwell in the house of the LORD all the days of my life, to gaze upon the beauty of the LORD and to inquire in his temple. For he will hide me in his shelter in the day of trouble; he will conceal me under the cover of his tent; he will lift me high upon a rock. And now my head shall be lifted up above my enemies all around me, and I will offer in his tent sacrifices with shouts of joy; I will sing and make melody to the LORD.*
>
> — Psalm 27.1–6

Hope Is Sustained through Diligently Seeking God

God calls us to search for Him. We must seek God's face. *You have said, 'Seek my face.' My heart says to you, 'Your face, LORD, do I seek.' Hide not your face from me. Turn not your servant away in anger, O you who have been my help. Cast me not off; forsake me not, O God of my salvation!* Psalm 27.8–9. How do we seek God? We seek God by preparing our minds for action, being sober in spirit, and hoping to the end, 1 Peter 1.13. We work to stay on top of our spiritual life. We prepare ourselves for spiritual labor. We realize the seriousness of our task. How we traverse in our earthly journey determines our spiritual destiny. **We have one fragile lifetime to do it.** Someone has said that the journey to heaven is not a sightseeing trip.

Our hope is sustained through living as obedient children who are not conformed to our former lifestyles. We follow through on our commitment to put on holiness, 1.14–15. Now, because we have been rescued from eternal death, our earnest desire is to be like Jesus. The extreme price that was paid in order to give us our hope is never far from the mind of a faithful child of God. ... *You were ransomed from the futile ways inherited from your forefathers, not with perishable things such as silver or gold, but with the precious blood of Christ, like that of a lamb without blemish or spot,* 1 Peter 1.18–19.

Conclusion:

Our hope is secure. It is based on God's word, which does not fail, 1 Peter 1.22–25. It is based upon God's promise for we serve a God who cannot lie, Titus 1.2. **As long as we diligently seek Him, we can be assured that nothing will separate us.** Both Paul and Peter affirmed this fact. *In all these things we are more than conquerors through him who loved us,* Romans 8.37. *Therefore, brothers, be all the more diligent to confirm your calling and election, for if you practice these qualities you will never fall. For in this way there will be richly provided for you an entrance into the eternal kingdom of our Lord and Savior Jesus Christ,* 2 Peter 1.10–11. **Where is your hope?**

For Thought and Reflection:

1. Define hope. How has God provided us with it?

2. What is the object of our hope?

3. How does Peter describe our reward?

4. How does the Holy Spirit play a role in our hope?

5. In what way do you think hope motivated Paul in his ministry to the Gentiles?

6. In Hebrews 6:19, what does the writer liken our hope to?

7. What are some things we must do to sustain our hope?

8. How secure is our hope?

9. Today's lesson has helped me become more assured of my salvation by:

The Proper Perspective on Obedience

Introduction:

The need for an obedient life as a response to our place and position in God's kingdom was highly stressed by Jesus and the apostles. Jesus expects those who come to Him to lead obedient lives. One of the most well-known passages regarding obedience is found in John 14.15: *If you love me, you will keep my commandments.* Others are:

- **Matthew 7.21-24** — *Not everyone who says to me, 'Lord, Lord,' will enter the kingdom of heaven, but the one who does the will of my Father who is in heaven. On that day many will say to me, 'Lord, Lord, did we not prophesy in your name, and cast out demons in your name, and do many mighty works in your name?' And then will I declare to them, 'I never knew you; depart from me, you workers of lawlessness.' Everyone then who hears these words of mine and does them will be like a wise man who built his house on the rock.*

- **Matthew 12.50** — *For whoever does the will of my Father in heaven is my brother and sister and mother.*

- **Luke 11.28** — *Blessed are those who hear the word of God and observe it.*

In their ministries, the apostles continued to stress the need for an obedient lifestyle.

- **1 Peter 1.15-16** — *as he who called you is holy, you also be holy in all your conduct, since it is written, "You shall be holy, for I am holy."*

- **1 Thessalonians 4.1b** — *… as you received from us how you ought to walk and to please God, just as you are doing, that you do so more and more.*

- **Hebrews 5.8-9** — *Although he was a son, he learned obedience through what he suffered. And being made perfect, he became the source of eternal salvation to all who obey him.*

Obedience is a central theme inside the New Testament. Our need for the possession of a lifestyle that submits to the headship of Jesus cannot be underemphasized. This is especially true as we can be impacted by a religious culture that stresses "just believe" and little else. **There is more to salvation than just a simple statement of belief that Jesus is our Savior.** The road to heaven is long, hard, and narrow, Matthew 7.13–14, and requires difficult decisions along the way. Each person has been called to *count the cost*, Luke 14.25–33, and live his or her life accordingly. We must preach on this matter without fear and honestly present the biblical contrast to the "easy-to-believe" mentality of our day.

However, it is important to evaluate the way we approach obedience. Many of us do a great job in expressing our need to respect the expectations of God. But, we must never neglect the need to communicate God's intention behind these actions. Following His commands is born out of something higher and more meaningful than just law-keeping. Through His revealed word, we can understand what God wants and respond through belief and obedience. Our obedience is the result of the relationship we have with Jesus. **While we obey God *because we have to*, we should be helping individuals progress to the point where they obey God *because they want to*.**

Aim Higher

So faith comes from hearing, and hearing through the word of Christ, Romans 10.17. Through His revealed word, we can understand what God wants and respond through belief and obedience. **God accepts only faith**. Faith is what motivates us to approach God in the manner He prescribes. We can't approach God by our own works. A person cannot do His own thing and expect God to accept it as service to Him. *There is a way that seems right to a man, but its end is the way to death*, Proverbs 14.12.

The need to abide by the expectations of Scripture in how we approach God in the work and worship of the church must not be ignored. But, we must never neglect the need to communicate God's intention behind these actions. **Our obedience has a purpose. God never asks us to direct our faith toward an illogical nothingness. God's righteousness is not arbitrary.** He expects us to follow through with a consciousness that we are depending solely on Him being true to His word. God is altogether trustworthy, and our exercise of faith toward Him is a demonstration of our recognition of this fact. Our devotion to God must spring from a heart that depends on Him. In Scripture, the heart is thought of as the basis of our thinking. It involves our mind, our will, and our source of knowledge. Jesus called our heart a "treasure," Matthew 12.35. This word refers to a "reservoir, storehouse, or box." Your heart is a storehouse. What is contained there will be expressed through your speech and actions.

Any service rendered to God must be offered with a connection to the heart. **That is, a heart that believes and wants to obey God.** While we should stress the importance of obedience, *we need to aim higher in our thinking process.* **Never forget the purpose of your service.** It should be a token of your love and devotion. It is a reflection of your love for our Lord. ***If you love me*, *you will keep my commandments*,** John 14.15 [emphasis mine]. **Commandment keeping *never* generates love for God.** But strong faith and trust in Him generate a desire to do what He says. This is why we must get to know God more, building our trust and confidence in His faithfulness to us. Do we share the devotion of Paul? See Philippians 3.7-11. When we truly know Him, we will never have a problem in compliance with His will.

From the beginning, God has always wanted our heart. Obeying God mechanically without the involvement of the heart results in wasted effort.

- **How is your heart?** *The sacrifices of God are a broken spirit; a broken and contrite heart, O God, you will not despise*, Psalm 51.17.

- **What has God always wanted?** *Wash yourselves; make yourselves clean; remove the evil of your deeds from before my eyes; cease to do evil, learn to do good; seek justice, correct oppression; bring justice to the fatherless, plead the widow's cause*, Isaiah 1.16–17.

Deity Is Not Dependent upon Us

We do not supply the needs of God. We can never offer Him something that He does not already own. We have nothing of value that is not already His. *Nor is He served by human hands, as though He needed anything, since He Himself gives to all mankind life and breath and everything,* Acts 17.25. Part of our obedience is learning how Jesus meets us as our servant in order to carry our burdens and supply us with His power.

When we became a Christian, we did not become His helper. Jesus did not hang out a "help wanted" sign, He hung out a "help available" sign.[36] Jesus does not need our help. He commands obedience and offers His help. He is our benefactor and servant, Mark 10.45. We come to God having nothing to offer, trade in, or purchase. He already owns every possession we have. He owns our money, time, resources, and life. When we work, it is only because He has given us life and everything. Our works never contribute to our salvation; they are a reflection of the saving work that Jesus has already done by the cross. We are who we are by *the grace of God,* 1 Corinthians 15.10. Our Lord is the ultimate servant-king. We walk in His shadow.

But, someone asks, "Didn't the apostles call themselves 'servants' of Christ?"

The simple answer is yes. Paul did so in Romans 1.1. Even Jesus calls us servants in other contexts, John 13.16. But this does not contradict the point I am trying to make. We are servants in the sense that we willingly surrender to His authority and His right to tell us whatever He pleases. We are not His servants in the sense that Jesus needs our help. **He is not dependent on us.** We are dependent on Him. Jesus uses every divine resource to help and strengthen us, guide and support us, and provide for our needs. In the next section, we'll see how this understanding can help us develop the proper perspective on obedience.

The Path to God Is Not through Externals

In chapter 8, we briefly discussed this fact. Some equate spirituality with rule keeping. Expectations are forced down the throats of individuals through the enforcement of external rules. **External rules do not make people spiritual.** We must reject a works-based approach to spiritual life and religious practice. We must resist the urge to turn our service to God and others into a check-list. Do you measure yourself by externals? Do you gauge your or someone else's spirituality by:

- Attendance at all services every Sunday.

- Attendance at mid-week Bible study.

- Regular contribution.

- Partaking of the Lord's Supper.

- Attendance at Bible classes and other special congregational events.

- Adherence to the "correct" set of beliefs, i.e., doctrinal compliance on *a cappella* singing, the one true church, and the work and role of the church, etc.

- Attempting to evangelize friends and family members.

It is implied that if this weekly check-list is not completed, favor is lost with God. The problem is not that the above activities should not be engaged in, **it is where the emphasis is placed**.

In one spiritual family, the need for weekly attendance at worship services and Bible class was so stressed that one new mother who gave birth early in the day on Sunday checked herself out of the hospital so she could be present at the evening service. Recalling her actions years later, she said she felt awful and was physically drained. But she had been so driven to the point of fear that she was afraid she would be lost if she missed the service that night.

Because of the continual focus on externals, some tend to operate first from the perspective of "checking off the box." In another spiritual family, the elders of the church called an assembly together for Sunday afternoon congregational singing. As he encouraged the family to participate in the service, one shepherd gently urged each member to be mindful of their spiritual commitment to *stir up one another to love and good works*, Hebrews 10.24. His point was that a person's presence that afternoon should have been a natural response of the heart, rising out of a love for God and fellow members of the body. One member completely missed the point. Thinking only of meeting an attendance requirement he told another family member:

"Well, I guess I have to go to that singing now—especially after that announcement."

The implication was that this person would rather be somewhere else, but they *had to go* to keep the spotlight off of them. While they may have been able to check off the box regarding their presence, **was God pleased with the motive or attitude?** This person might as well have stayed home.

The approach to God is never through external actions, **it is through the heart!**

Our relationship with God is not based on a pay-as-you-go system. No person earns anything from God through spiritual acts of service. Attendance at worship services, giving, doctrinal correctness, and evangelism are not conducted in order to gain favor with God, **they are the fruit of a successful relationship with God.**

This is not a new phenomenon. Mankind's tendency to stress external actions as the primary approach to God goes all the way back to the Israelites under the law of Moses. **Vigorous activity in the name of God does not automatically guarantee acceptance by our Creator.**

The Old Testament examples are plentiful.

- **Isaiah 1.11** — *What to me is the multitude of your sacrifices? …I have had enough of burnt offerings of rams and the fat of well-fed beasts; I do not delight in the blood of bulls, or of lambs, or of goats.*

- **Jeremiah 6.20b** — *Your burnt offerings are not acceptable, nor your sacrifices pleasing to me.*

- **Malachi 1.10** — *Oh that there were one among you who would shut the doors, that you might not kindle fire on my altar in vain! I have no pleasure in you, says the Lord of hosts, and I will not accept an offering from your hand.*

- **Isaiah 66.3** — *He who slaughters an ox is like one who kills a man; he who sacrifices a lamb, like one who breaks a dog's neck; he who presents a grain offering, like one who offers pig's blood; he who makes a memorial offering of frankincense, like one who blesses an idol …*

- **1 Samuel 15.22** — *Has the Lord as great delight in burnt offerings and sacrifices, as in obeying the voice of the Lord? Behold, to obey is better than sacrifice, and to listen than the fat of rams.*

In the New Testament, the teachings of Jesus speak to us:

- **Matthew 7.21-23** — *Not everyone who says to me, 'Lord, Lord,' will enter the kingdom of heaven, but the one who does the will of my Father who is in heaven. On that day many will say to me, 'Lord, Lord, did we not prophesy in your name, and cast out demons in your name, and do many mighty works in your name?' And then will I declare to them, 'I never knew you; depart from me, you workers of lawlessness.'*

- **Luke 18.9-14** — *He also told this parable to some who trusted in themselves that they were righteous, and treated others with contempt: 'Two men went up into the temple to pray, one a Pharisee and the other a tax collector. The Pharisee, standing by himself, prayed thus: "God, I thank you that I am not like other men, extortioners, unjust, adulterers, or even like this tax collector. I fast twice a week; I give tithes of all that I get." But the tax collector, standing far off, would not even lift up his eyes to heaven, but beat his breast, saying, "God, be merciful to me, a sinner!" I tell you, this man went down to his house justified, rather than the other. For everyone who exalts himself will be humbled, but the one who humbles himself will be exalted.'*

These examples shout from the pages on which they are written. Are we listening? We must guard against our own tendency to stress the external actions of Christianity over the changed heart behind the activity. One may do many things for Christ, abide by His rules, and still be lost. **Any service rendered to God without the action of a changed heart is useless**. Some are *clean in their own eyes, but are not washed of their filth,* Proverbs 30.12.

In every dispensation, **God has made it clear that salvation is not derived through law keeping**. No law can give life, Galatians 3.21. And yet, we still fight the tendency to do otherwise. Some believe the answer for strengthening weak Christians is to be found through increased attendance of worship services. Yet, there are many who come to church every week who do not truly know God. Some give thousands of dollars to the church and the needy, but still aren't connected with Him. **The way to God is not through *doing more*.** Rather, it is through a surrendered heart that is learning *not to rely on ourselves, but on God who raises the dead,* 2 Corinthians 1.9.

This is where it all begins. Our heart must desire *God.* Our heavenly Father desires to have fellowship with us. He desires our love. *Everyone who believes that Jesus is the Christ has been born of God, and everyone who loves the Father loves whoever has been born of him,* 1 John 5.1. It is characteristic of any believer to love God and Christ. Do we move with holy affection? This desire for relationship with God is basic to salvation. We have been *called into the fellowship of his Son, Jesus Christ our Lord,* 1 Corinthians 1.9. **Any activity offered in God's name is useless without a *relationship* with Him.**

What Happens When We Operate from the Proper Perspective?

When we come to understand the pathway to God is not found through externals, we must never conclude that externals are unnecessary. The activity of our spiritual service is the result of a changed heart that has an active relationship with God. Every good work we do has been created by God so that we should walk in them, bringing glory to God, Ephesians 2.10. What does life look like when our heart is connected to God?

We will be sensitive to sin. *We walk in the light as He Himself is in the light ...* 1 John 1.7. We understand that if we are going to have fellowship with God that we have to be holy. When sin occurs in our life, we understand it must be confessed. We do not have to sin. But when we do, we know to whom to go—Jesus Christ—our Advocate, 1 John 2.1–3. The person who is truly converted will be sensitive to the sinful realities in life. Isn't that the example Paul set for us in Romans 7.14–25? How does this apply to you? Are you aware of the spiritual battle raging within you? Do you realize that to have true communion with God, you have to have a holy life? You can not walk in darkness and claim to have fellowship with Him.

We will live in obedience to God's word. *And by this we know that we have come to know him, if we keep his commandments. Whoever says 'I know him' but does not keep his commandments is a liar, and the truth is not in him,* 1 John 2.3–4. "Keep" as used in 2.3, speaks of watchful, careful, and thoughtful obedience. **It involves not only the act of obedience, but also the spirit of obedience.** It involves a willing, habitual safeguarding of God's word—*not just in letter but in spirit.* If you desire to obey God's word out of gratitude for all that Christ has done for you, and if you see that desire producing an overall pattern of obedience, you can be assured that you are operating from the proper perspective.

We will reject this evil world. *Do not love the world or the things in the world. If anyone loves the world, the love of the Father is not in him,* 1 John 2.15. "The world" refers to false religion, crime, immorality, materialism, etc. We must develop the type of heart that repels these things. While sometimes we may be lured into these things, it isn't what we love; it's what we hate. That's the way Paul felt when he fell into sin, Romans 7.15. As frustrating as it is to succumb to sin, our hearts must be characterized by a transformation that loves the things of God more than the things of this world. It is our love for Him that will draw us out and redirect our focus toward heavenly priorities. Will you reject the world?

We will eagerly await Christ's return. *Beloved, we are God's children now, and what we will be has not yet appeared; but we know that when he appears* *we shall be like him, because we shall see him as he is. And everyone who thus hopes in him purifies himself as he is pure,* 1 John 3.2–3. The Christian's hope is fixed on Christ's return. Our *citizenship is in heaven,* Philippians 3.20. Are you waiting for that? Does it excite you to know that one day you will be set free from this fleshly body of sin and given new life? *Just as we have borne the image of the man of dust, we shall also bear the image of the man of heaven,* 1 Corinthians 15.49. Hopeful living provides the motivation to make positive changes in our life. Longing for Christ's return is an indication of a heart that is connected with God.

We will see a decreasing pattern of sin in our life.

> *Everyone who makes a practice of sinning also practices lawlessness; sin is lawlessness. You know that he appeared in order to take away sins, and in him there is no sin. No one who abides in him keeps on sinning; no one who keeps on sinning has either seen him or known him. Little children, let no one deceive you. Whoever practices righteousness is righteous, as he is righteous. Whoever makes a practice of sinning is of the devil, for the devil has been sinning from the beginning. The reason the Son of God appeared was to destroy the works of the devil. No one born of God makes a practice of sinning, for God's seed abides in him, and he cannot keep on sinning because he has been born of God.*
>
> — 1 John 3.4–9

Sin as a life pattern is incompatible with salvation. Christians are no longer slaves to sin. We have offered ourselves as servants to the Lord, Romans 6.14, 17–18. We are working to break the habit of sin and move closer to the Lord.

Conclusion:

What does this mean to us personally? Paul describes it in Galatians 2.20: *I have been crucified with Christ. It is no longer I who live, but Christ who lives in me. And the life I now live in the flesh I live by faith in the Son of God, who loved me and gave himself for me.* This verse is not just a cold fact. Rather

it is something that we should experience. We come to God no longer depending on ourselves, but rather on Him who supplies us all things. This is the essence of brokenness. It is the expression of total trust. It is the expression of a heart that is driven by the realization of the need to be with Him because there is no other way. Paul said, *But far be it for me to boast except in the cross of our Lord Jesus Christ, by which the world has been crucified to me, and I to the world,* Galatians 6.14.

There is something to be enjoyed in knowing God intimately. In John 10.10, Jesus did not say, *I have come that you have life.* Rather, He said, *I have come that you may have life,* **and have it abundantly** [emphasis mine]. By adding that life can be abundant, Jesus moves us into the realm of experience. The Christian life is a rich life of spiritual blessing. We are meant to enjoy peace, love, joy, and purpose. Our fellowship with Him promises:

- **Comfort** — 2 Corinthians 1.3.
- **Grace** — 1 Peter 5.10.
- **The supply of all our needs** — Philippians 4.19.
- **Teaching and edification** — Ephesians 5.19.
- **The blessing of intimate closeness with God** — Romans 8.15.
- **A source of help during times of trouble** — Hebrews 4.16.

Are you approaching God with the proper perspective on obedience?

For Thought and Reflection:

1. Why is a proper perspective on obedience so important as we live inside today's culture?

2. How does John 14.15 express the purpose of obedience?

3. Why is it important to understand that we do not supply any need to God?

4. How do we know vigorous activity in the name of God does not guarantee acceptance by God?

5. What is the way to God?

6. Why is a relationship with God so important?

7. What can you do to become more sensitive to sin?

8. What is communicated by the word *keep* in 1 John 2.3?

9. How can you strengthen your love for God while diminishing your love for the world?

10. What should be the life pattern developing in your life? What is this a reflection of?

11. How does an obedient heart move us toward intimacy with God?

12. What does an obedient life produce?

Comfort in Christ

Introduction:

In January 2001, President Bill Clinton spent the final weeks of his eight year presidency preparing to leave office. As it is a custom, his desk was covered with numerous pardon requests from individuals all over the country seeking jail time to be reduced or removed, and/or felony records to be expunged. One of the most notorious pardons the President granted was for Marc Rich who had been indicted on tax evasion. Rich hid over $48 million from the IRS and was charged with 51 counts of tax fraud. He was also accused of running illegal oil deals with Iran during the 1979-1980 Iranian hostage crisis. At the time of the pardon, Rich was living in Switzerland, having fled the United States during the prosecution of his case. It was suspected by Clinton's political enemies that Rich's ex-wife, Denise, had paid off the Clintons, as she had been a heavy contributor to the Democrat Party and Clinton's Presidential campaigns. Clinton was investigated to see if there was any wrong doing on his part, but no evidence was found to bring charges against him.[837]

Bill Clinton's pardon of Marc Rich is not the first Presidential pardon that Americans have viewed with skepticism. George H. W. Bush pardoned Casper Wineberger early in his presidency, effectively ending any more investigation into the 1980's Iran-Contra Scandal. We tend to cynically view Presidential pardons of this manner because the offender's attitude and actions suggest they are not sorry for their transgression. Have they really changed?

Thinking of this example, ask yourself as to what viewpoint you view God's forgiveness. The way God forgives is not equal to a Presidential pardon. When we come to Christ, indicating our deep need for Him to save us from our sin, God goes to work within us, helping us change who we are. "God's work of forgiveness is much more active and transforming than simply passing a sentence. Our forgiveness is not some judicial fiction, but a reality being worked out in our lives by the Holy Spirit."[38] God's forgiveness changes us inside and out. It has the power to change our heart.

How many New Testament Christians live life from the perspective that they will just have to *hope for the best* on judgment day? There is little assurance or confidence in their day-to-day life because they have told themselves it might be presumptuous to expect salvation. When dwelling on heaven or eternal rest they quickly move their thoughts back to their need for personal responsibility in doing all they can do to get to heaven. If we live only from the perspective of personal responsibility, it tends to lead us to focus on our shortcomings. All we can see is the way our thoughts and behaviors do not add up. This results in a lack of confidence. It produces fear that says God is constantly displeased with the way we live life.

At this point, you may be thinking that personal responsibility is absolutely required. You know the Scriptures as well as I do. Philippians 2.12, Matthew 7.21–23, and 1 Peter 1.13–16 all come to mind. There are certainly others. We must heed the instruction in these passages. But it is important to understand this is not the only perspective from which to view the Christian life. It is perfectly acceptable, and even encouraged in Scripture, that we regularly view our spiritual life from the lens of comfort and assurance. God has forgiven us and nothing can separate us from His love:

> For I am sure that neither death nor life, nor angels nor rulers, nor things present nor things to come, nor powers, nor height nor depth, nor anything else in all creation, will be able to separate us from the love of God in Christ Jesus our Lord.
>
> — Romans 8:38–39

How often do you focus on the message of hope and assurance? We need to do this more. The lack of confidence that produces fear may have led some to the point of spiritual paralysis. Their guilt and fear have morphed into a huge burden of guilt. The burden is so large that they may feel it is useless to continue because there is no way to get away from the past. In this, they have become their own worst enemy. This is not the kind of spiritual life God intends for His children to live.

When Your Conscience Weighs on You, Turn to Your Father

First century Christians dealt with many of the same fears and doubts we experience. In his epistle, John rightly deals with the concept of personal responsibility. The epistle contains very rigid tests that define, determine, and designate what it means to be a disciple of Jesus. For example:

- **1.5–6 — Christians do not walk in darkness.** Christians walk in the light and do not live like the world.

- **1.9 — Christians confess sin.** We must be quick to get our sin out in the open before God.

- **2.3 — Christians keep commandments by obeying His word.**

- **2.9 — Christians love the brethren.** If not, they walk in darkness.

- **2.15 — If Christians love the world, the love of the Father is not in them.** What could be more of a black and white statement?

- **2.16-17 — Christians do not love what is in the world.** We do not love what is passing away.

- **2.29 — Christians practice righteousness by following a righteous pattern.** This pattern is Jesus Himself.

- **3.6 — Christians do not *keep on sinning*.**

- **3.14-18 — Christians actively demonstrate brotherly love through their actions.**

- **3.22; 4.7–8; and 5.13 contain similar absolutes.**

After reading through this list, we might be tempted to conclude that only those with a perfect love for God and others as well as perfect obedience to every command are the only ones with any hope. This standard stops us in our tracks. *What human measures up?* Is your obedience perfect? Do you still battle an attraction to this world? Do you fight the lust of the flesh, the eyes, and the pride of life? Are you locked in an addiction to things that are passing away?

1 John 2.1 provides relief from the absolutes of God's standard. *My little children, I am writing these things to you so that you may not sin. But **if anyone does sin**, we have an advocate with the Father, Jesus Christ the righteous* [emphasis mine]. In the original language, *if* carries along with it, possibility. We could easily say, *if … and you will … sin, you have an advocate with the Father, Jesus Christ the righteous.* While John encourages Christians to choose not to engage in the practice of sin, when we do sin, we have someone who will come stand by our side to plead our case. Long after initial salvation, we can and do sin, 1.8, 10. We need to be willing to admit the reality of human frailty and Satan's seductive power.

We have committed to keeping His commandments and abiding in Him, 2.3, 5, 6a. We imitate Jesus by walking in the same manner as He walked, 2.6b. But, we do have shortcomings and imperfections. Our obedience is not always perfect. Thus, Jesus is the propitiation for our sins, 2.2a. As we realize our shortcomings and imperfections we strive to cast them off because we are committed to becoming more like Jesus. God promises to partner with us as we walk in righteousness. We walk, not to be saved, but because we are saved.

> *For by grace you have been saved through faith. And this is not your own doing; it is the gift of God, not a result of works, so that no one may boast. For we are his workmanship, created in Christ Jesus for good works, which God prepared beforehand, that we should walk in them.*
>
> — Ephesians 2.8–10

Still, fear and doubts will confront us. We will wrestle with our conscience because we know we have not met and cannot meet all of God's standards. At times it feels Satan lurks in every corner and at every turn. But yet, John offers assurance: *By this we shall know that we are of the truth and reassure our heart before him; for whenever our heart condemns us, God is greater than our heart, and he knows everything,* 1 John 3.19–20.

God knows us better than we know ourselves. He sees our heart. "He knows that our often weak attempts to keep His commands spring from a true allegiance to Him."[39] You have entrusted your soul to a merciful God. This should set your heart at rest. God will always welcome and forgive the person who seeks His forgiveness and is dedicated to a relationship with Him. God's firm foundation stands, bearing this seal: *'The Lord knows those who are his,'* and, *'Let everyone who names the name of the Lord depart from iniquity,'* 2 Timothy 2:19.

When our conscience is weighing on us, we must turn to our spiritual Father. We have free access to the throne. Consider the following passages:

- **Hebrews 4.16** — *Let us then with confidence draw near to the throne of grace, that we may receive mercy and find grace to help in time of need.*

- **1 John 5.14** — *And this is the confidence that we have toward him, that if we ask anything according to his will he hears us.*

- **Psalm 139.23–24** — *Search me, O God, and know my heart! Try me and know my thoughts! And see if there be any grievous way in me, and lead me in the way everlasting!*

When we come to God, He will show us mercy, comfort us, and reassure us that we are His children. Those who follow God from the heart can know they belong to God and put their hearts at rest.

> *Beloved, if our heart does not condemn us, we have confidence before God; and whatever we ask we receive from him, because we keep his commandments and do what pleases him. And this is his commandment, that we believe in the name of his Son Jesus Christ and love one another, just as he has commanded us. Whoever keeps his commandments abides in God, and God in him. And by this we know that he abides in us, by the Spirit whom he has given us.*
>
> — 1 John 3:21–24

A New Outlook on Life

As Christians, we are no longer defined by our guilt. We are defined by righteousness. *For our sake he made him to be sin who knew no sin, so that in him we might become the righteousness of God,* 2 Corinthians 5.21.

We live under a new reality. We have been liberated from sin! We are no longer oppressed by guilt. We have been sanctified. We are holy and righteous! "God's forgiveness is not just a change in verdict; it contains the power to actually enable us to live differently."[40] We have been liberated and can now go about doing God's work without fear of condemnation. We are being transformed into the image of Christ: *Now the Lord is the Spirit, and where the Spirit of the Lord is, there is freedom. And we all, with unveiled face, beholding the glory of the Lord, are being transformed into the same image from one degree of glory to another. For this comes from the Lord who is the Spirit,* 2 Corinthians 3.17–18.

Conclusion:

From what perspective do you view your spiritual life? Do you find yourself battling doubts and uncertainty? Take those things to God. If there is sin in your life, confess it. Get it in the open before the Lord and seek His forgiveness. God will forgive you. Once you have done that, trust God's word for what it says. You have been forgiven. Rejoice in this fact and take comfort in it. Praise God for His great love for us!

> *Who shall separate us from the love of Christ? Shall tribulation, or distress, or persecution, or famine, or nakedness, or danger, or sword? As it is written, 'For your sake we are being killed all the day long; we are regarded as sheep to be slaughtered.' No, in all these things we are more than conquerors through him who loved us.*
>
> — Romans 8.35–37

For Thought and Reflection:

1. Have you ever felt it might be presumptuous to expect salvation? Why?

2. What do we tend to focus on more: personal responsibility or the message of hope and assurance found throughout the New Testament?

3. How would you define spiritual paralysis?

4. In what ways does John emphasize personal responsibility in 1 John?

5. What is a disciple?

6. How can we find comfort in 1 John 2.1-3 and 3.19-20?

7. If our conscience weighs on us, what should we do?

8. By what is a Christian defined?

9. How can this new definition give you a better outlook on life?

10. What does God do for us as we go to work in His kingdom?

End Notes

[1] Charles, R. H. (1913). *The Martyrdom of Isaiah. In Apocrypha and Pseudepigrapha of Old Testament.* Oxford: Clarendon Press.

[2] Pratte, D. (2006). *Grace of God, Mercy, Works, Law, Obedience, and Salvation in the Bible.* Retrieved October 8, 2009, from Gospel Way: www.gospelway.com

[3] MacArthur, J. (1986). *The Beatitudes.* Retrieved October 8, 2009, from Happy Are the Merciful: www.biblebb.com/files/mac/sg2202.htm

[4] Spurgeon, C. (1883). "The Doctrines of Grace Do Not Lead to Sin." Retrieved 06/27/2013 from http://www.spurgeon.com/sermons/1735.htm

[5] MacArthur J. (1993). *Saving Grace, Pt. 1.* Retrieved 07/18/2012 from http://www.gty.org/resources/sermons/56-18/saving-grace-part-1

[6] Lockhart, J. (2012). "Why I Am Faithful." *Spiritual Sword.* July 2012. 43:4. p.48.

[7] Turner, R. F. (1989). *Sermons on Grace.* Temple Terrace, FL: Florida College Bookstore.

[8] Bonhoeffer, D. (1963). *The Cost of Discipleship.* New York: Macmillan.

[9] Monergism.com. Retrieved 8/2/2012 from http://www.monergism.com/thethreshold/articles/onsite/qna/easybelieve.html

[10] Bonhoeffer: *The Cost of Discipleship.*

[11] MacArthur, J. (2013). *Our Divine Advocate.* Retrieved 06/20/2013 from http://www.gty.org/resources/print/sermons/62-9.

[12] Chadwell, D. (2004). *Understanding Justification.*

[13] Everett, J. (1999). *Walk in the Light.* Cedar Park Church of Christ Bulletin. Retrieved 4/18/2012 from http://www.cedarparkchurchofchrist.org/bulletin/1999/bull075.htm

[14] Everett, J. (1999). See previous footnote.

[15] Chadwell.

[16] MacArthur, J. (2002). *The Certainty of Sin, Pt. 3*. Grace to You. Retrieved 4/17/2012 from http://www.gty.org/resources/sermons/62-7/the-certainty-of-sin-part-3

[17] Getty, K. Townend, S. (2001). *In Christ Alone*. Song Lyrics. Kingsway Music.

[18] Jackson, J. (2006, June 23). *What is Propitiation?* Retrieved October 5, 2006, from Christian Courier.com: www.christiancourier.com/articles/print/what_is_ propitiation

[19] Piper, J. (2002). *Let us Walk in the Light of God. Desiring God*. Retrieved 4/12/2012 from http://www.desiringgod.org/resource-library/sermons/let-us-walk-in-the-light-of-god

[20] Ellis, J. (2012). Romans 3.21-4.25: Justified by grace thru faith without deeds of law. *The Power of Grace*. Retrieved July 1, 2012 from http://joelellis.blogspot. com/2012/05/romans-321-425-justified-through-faith.html

[21] Chadwell, D. (1986). "Having the Faith of Abraham." Nashville: 21st Century Christian.

[22] Cranfield, C. E. B. (1985). *Romans: A Shorter Commentary*. Edinburg, Scotland. T & T Clark. 292.

[23] I found this story in remarks made by John MacArthur. He says this quote came from Barnhouse's Commentary on Romans. To access MacArthur's writing, go here: http://www.gty.org/resources/sermons/45-39/salvation-by-divine-powernot-human-effort

[24] See Edwin Crozier's excellent writing on the lame beggar in Acts 3: http:// edwincrozier.com/2013/02/25/the-lame-beggar-of-acts-3-a-picture-of-gods-grace/

[25] Stanley, C. (1990). *Eternal Security: Can You Be Sure?* Nashville. Thomas Nelson. 74.

[26] Stanley, p. 80.

[27] Bethke, J. (2012). "Why Jesus Doesn't Want You to 'Ask Him Into Your Heart.'" Jefferson Bethke Blog. Retrieved 06/27/2013 from http://www.jeffbethke.com/ why-jesus-doesnt-want-you-to-ask-him-into-your-heart

[28] Spurgeon, C. (1883). "The Doctrines of Grace Do Not Lead to Sin." Retrieved 06/25/2013 from http://www.spurgeon.org/sermons/1735.htm

[29] MacArthur, J. (1996.) "Free From Sin, Pt. 1." Grace to You. Retrieved 06/25/2013 from http://www.gty.org/resources.print/sermons/45-48

[30] Ray, M. (2012). "That Form of Doctrine, Pt. 1." To Proclaim Wondrous Deeds. Retrieved 07/03/2013 from http://www.maxdray.com/2012/07/14/that-form-of-doctrine-i

[31] Clarke, A. (1836). *A Commentary on the Whole Bible.* Electronic Copy. OakTree Software, ver. 1.6.

[32] The "quotes" in this passage are from MacArthur. See previous citation.

[33] West, M. (2013). "Hello My Name Is." Songs of Southside Independent Music Publishing. External Combustion Music. Songs for Delaney. Retrieved 06/25/2013 from: http://www.klove.com/music/artists/matthew-west/songs/hello,-my-name-is-lyrics.aspx

[34] MacArthur, J. (1983). "The Spirit Confirms Our Adoption." *Grace To You.* Retrieved 08/08/2012 from http://www.gty.org/resources/sermons/45-59/the-spirit-confirms-our-adoption/

[35] Hamilton C. D. (1995). *1 Peter.* Bowling Green, KY: Guardian of Truth Foundation.

[36] Piper, J. (1995). *The Blinding Effects of Serving God. Desiring God.* Retrieved 06/25/2013 from http://www.desiringgod.org/resource-library/sermons/the-blinding-effects-of-serving-god

[37] Dell, K., & Myers, R. (2007). *The 10 Most Notorious Presidential Pardons.* Retrieved 12/10/2009 from Time.com: http://www.time.com/time/2007/presidentia-pardons/10.html

[38] Benjamin, C. (2004). *Your Sins Are Forgiven.* Retrieved 12/10/2009 from Westark Church of Christ: http://www.westarkchurchofchrist.org/benjamin/2004/040208am.htm

[39] Marshall, I. H. (1978). *The Epistles of John.* Grand Rapids, MI: Eerdmans. 178.

[40] Benjamin. See previous citation.

More Bible Study workbooks that you can order from Spiritbuilding.com or your favorite Christian bookstore.

Inside Out (Carl McMurray)
Studying spiritual growth in bite-sized pieces
Night and Day (Andrew Roberts)
Comparing New Testament Christianity and Islam
Church Discipline (Royce DeBerry)
A study on an important responsibility for the Lord's church
Exercising Authority (John Baughn)
How we use and understand authority on a daily basis
Compass Points (Carl McMurray)
22 foundation lessons for home studies, prospects, or new Christians
We're Different Because... (Carl McMurray)
A workbook on authority and recent church history
Communing with the Lord (Matthew Allen)
A study of the Lord's Supper & issues surrounding it
Parenting Through the Ages (Royce & Cindy DeBerry)
Bible principles tested & explained by successful parents
Marriage Through the Ages (Royce & Cindy DeBerry)
A quarter's study of God's design for this part of our life
What Should I Do? (Dennis Tucker)
A study that seeks Bible answers to life's important questions
How To Study the Bible (Jeff Archer)
25 lessons on how to study & understand the Bible
From Fear to Faith (Matthew Allen)
Coming to grips with the doctrine of grace
The Messiah's Misfits (Bryan Nash)
A study of the apostles of Jesus Christ
Living a Spirit Filled Life (Matthew Allen)
A study of Galatians & Ephesians with practical applications
The Lion Is the Lamb (Andrew Roberts)
A study of the King of Kings, His glorious kingdom, & His promised return
When Opportunity Knocks (Matthew Allen)
Lessons on how to meet the J.W./Mormon who knocks on your door
The Last Mile of the Way (Kipp Campbell)
A workbook study of the last week of the Messiah's life
Ancient Choices for Modern Dilemmas (John Baughn)
Biblical view of the modern family, current culture, and American politics
In Search of Christian Confidence (John Baughn)
A study to help one find the confidence God intended for His people

More Bible Study workbooks that you can order from Spiritbuilding.com or your favorite Christian bookstore.

Textual Studies

The Parables, Taking a Deeper Look (Kipp Campbell)
A detailed look at our Lord's teaching stories
That I May Know Him (Aaron Kemple) Vol. 1 & 2
A chronological study of the life of Christ in a harmony of the gospels
1st Corinthians study guide (Chad Sychtysz)
Studies to take the student through this important letter
2nd Corinthians study guide (Chad Sychtysz)
Studies to take the student through this important letter
Hebrews study guide (Chad Sychtysz)
Studies to take the student through this important letter
Romans study guide (Chad Sychtysz)
Studies to take the student through this important letter
Galatians study guide (Chad Sychtysz)
Studies to take the student through this important letter
Ephesian study guide (Chad Sychtysz)
Studies to take the student through this important letter
Philippian, Colossians, Philemon study guide (Chad Sychtysz)
Studies to take the student through these important letters
1 & 2 Timothy and Titus (Matthew Allen)
A commentary workbook on these letters from Paul
Faith in Action: Studies in James (Mike Wilson)
Bible class workbook and commentary on James
From Beneath the Altar (Carl McMurray)
A workbook commentary on the Book of Revelation

1 Samuel & 2 Samuel (Matthew Allen)
Studying the life and times of this prophet, priest, & judge
Proverbs, Wisdom for Dummies (Carl McMurray)
A workbook study including every verse in Proverbs, divided into topics
An Overview of Isaiah (Chad Sychtysz)
A workbook study of this messianic prophet
An Overview of Jeremiah (Chad Sychtysz)
A workbook study of this prophet
Esteemed of God, Studying the Book of Daniel (Carl McMurray)
Covering the man as well as the time between the testaments
The Minor Prophets, Vol. 1 & 2 (Matthew Allen)
Old lessons that speak directly to us today

Special Interest

The AD 70 Doctrine (Morris Bowers)
The truth about Realized Eschatology
The Holy Spirit of God (Chad Sychtysz)
A diligent, thorough study of this important subject
The Gospel of Forgiveness (Chad Sychtysz)
A presentation of this subject from different biblical angles
Letters to Young Preachers (Warren Berkley)
Letters from older preachers to younger on what they face
Behind the Preacher's Door (Warren Berkley and Mark Roberts)
Issues that preachers will have to deal with
Seeking the Sacred (Chad Sychtysz)
How to know God the way that HE wants us to know Him
Will You Wipe My Tears? (Joyce Jamerson)
Wisdom & resources to teach us how to help others through sorrow

Studies for Women

I Will NOT Be Lukewarm (Dana Burk)
A ladies study on defeating mediocrity
Reveal in Me... (Jeanne Sullivan)
A study to assist ladies in discovering and developing their talents
Will You Wipe My Tears? (Joyce Jamerson)
Wisdom & resources to teach us how to help others through sorrow
Bridges or Barriers (Cindy DeBerry & Angie Kmitta)
Study encouraging harmony with younger/older sisters-in-Christ
Learning to Sing at Midnight (Joanne Beckley)
A study book about spiritual growth benefiting women of all ages
Re-charging Your Prayer Life (Lonnie Cruse)
Workbook for any woman wanting a richer prayer life
Does This Armor Make Me Look Fat? (Lonnie Cruse)
A study of the Christian armor and how it fits women
Heading for Harvest (Joyce Jamerson)
A study of the fruit of the Spirit
Behind Every Good Man (Joyce Jamerson)
Studying the women that stand behind faithful men of today
Forgotten Womanhood (Joanne Beckley)
Studying the traits of godly womanhood
Look Into Your Heart (Joyce Jamerson)
Studying how to calm one's heart, to develop one that is God approved

Studies for Young People

The Purity Pursuit (Andrew Roberts)
Helping teens achieve purity in all aspects of life
Paul's Letter to the Romans (Matthew Allen)
Putting righteousness by faith on a young person's level
Snapshots, Defining Moments in a Girl's Life (Nicole Sardinas)
How to make godly decisions when it really matters
The Path of Peace (Cassondra Givans)
Relevant and important topics of study for teens
Transitions (Ken Weliever)
A relevant life study for this changing age group
A Christian's Approach to... (Cougan Collins)
Studies that deal with the issues of life
God's Plan for Dating and Marriage (Dennis Tucker)
Considering God's directions in this vital area
Back to the Beginning (Cougan Collins)
Studying the book of Genesis
A Christian's Approach to... (Cougan Collins)
Dealing with the issues of this life
Compass Points (Carl McMurray)
22 foundation lessons for home studies or new Christians
Eye to Eye with Women of the Bible (Joanne Beckley)
Studies for girls of biblical women, good and bad
The Gospel and You (Andrew Roberts)
Helping teens achieve and possess their own saving faith
We're Different Because... (Carl McMurray)
A workbook on authority and recent church history

**Try any of these study workbooks in the
LIVING LETTER SERIES by Frank Jamerson**

The Gospel of Mark / The Gospel of John / Acts
The Letter to the Romans / 1 Corinthians / 2 Corinthians
The Letter to the Galatians / The Letter to the Ephesians
Philippians and Colossians / 1 & 2 Timothy & Titus
1 & 2 Thessalonians / The Letter to the Hebrews
The Letter of James /1 Peter / 2 Peter and Jude / 1-2-3 John

Other Bible Study Workbooks by Frank Jamerson
The Godhead / Lord, Please Teach Us to Give!
A Study of the New Testament Church
Bible Authority, How Established How Applied
Elders & Deacons...and Their Wives

www.ingramcontent.com/pod-product-compliance
Lightning Source LLC
Chambersburg PA
CBHW020949030426
42339CB00004B/19